FOIL
Cookery

Lori Herod

Illustrations by Janet S. Ballard

Paradise Cay Publications, Inc.
Arcata, California

FOIL COOKERY

Copyright © 2007 by Lorena Herod

Published by
Paradise Cay Publications, Inc., P. O. Box 29, Arcata, CA 95518-0029
(800) 736-4509 Phone; (707) 822-9163 Fax
paracay@humboldt1.com

Cover design by Rob Johnson, www.johnsondesign.org
Cover photograph courtesy of the Reynolds Kitchens.

Third Edition, 2007
Printed in the United States of America

ISBN 978-0-939837-77-3

Limits of Liability and Disclaimer of Warranty

DEDICATION

I would like to dedicate the latest vesion of *Foil Cookery* to my husband, Wayne, for encouraging me on my many camping weekends testing recipes.

As a proud parent and grandparent, I also dedicate this book to my four children—Kim, Amy and John, Becky and Chris, Andrew and Nicole—and eight grandchildren—Jordan, Megan, Tanner, Lauren, Cooper, Lucy, Ryann, and Charles—who are a constant source of pride and love.

I must also mention my dear friend Carma, who in the early years packed up her two children and with my children we would head off to one of Missouri's beautiful State Campgrounds. We had so much fun hiking and exploring what each state park had to offer. Little did we know what an impact these trips would have in providing lasting memories for us as well as for our children.

AUTHOR

Lorena I. Herod has been an avid camper for many years. In *Foil Cookery* she brings us her observations and experiences from many memorable excursions. As a Girl Scout leader in Kansas City, Missouri she was an active participant in leadership and winter survival training programs. Lorena has also taken an active role as a Boy Scout Troop outdoor cooking consultant. She provided demonstrations and hands-on training using a number of cooking techniuqes including foil cooking. Added to the cooking methods, Lorena has demonstrated and provided hands-on training with selecting different cooking fuels and their proper use. With the publication of this book, Lorena hopes to pass on her passion, love, respect, and admiration for nature.

GRAPHIC ILLUSTRATOR

Janet S. Ballard has a B.S. degree in Art Education and an M.S. degree in Instructional Technology from Kansas State University. She has taught on the university level as well as in public schools for 27 years. With funding from a federal grant, Janet created a series of graphics used by the Kansas State Restaurant Management Department for training purposes. She has also created many illustrations used on elementary grade cards, a logo design used by the school/business alliance, and several designs for a school district Arts Festival. Janet has sculpted and painted symbols used on award plaques presently hanging in four military museums, one as far away as Australia. At the present time, Janet is a high school art teacher in the Park Hill School District of Kansas City, Missouri. While fulfilling her teaching duties, she does commission character drawings, house portraits, and pen and ink architectural drawings.

CONTENTS

Preface

Winter, spring, summer or fall—whatever the season—Mother Nature is on stage for your enjoyment. Her splendor ranges from the serenity of a cool brook to the wild savagery of a mountain river cutting through canyons, seemingly racing against time; from the almost endless flatland of the heartland prairies to the majesty of mountain ranges reaching for the sky; from the myriad of rivers lacing the countryside to the swells of the oceans' tide. This is nature's "theme park" at your disposal.

The costs are minimal and the memories will last a lifetime. As we drink in nature's treasure, our obligation and responsibility is to leave it undisturbed for generations beyond our lifetime. The countless hours that I have spent writing and testing recipes for this book have been some of the most enjoyable of my life. It is my sincere wish that *Foil Cookery* will offer you new-found time through easy cooking so that you can enjoy your camping experiences to their fullest.

COOKING WITH FIRE

Fire is man's friend but it can also be his enemy. Any fire no matter how small, under the right conditions, can become a raging fire consuming hundreds, if not thousands of acres. To make sure you aren't the one responsible for such devastation, douse the fire with at least two buckets of water and stir the ashes as you do so.

A crackling fire seems to attract people and draw them closer. Fires seem to have a calming effect on even the most frazzled of nerves. Have you ever noticed that when people are gathered around a campfire, thoughts go from pleasant remembrances of the past to plans and dreams for the future? Sitting around the campfire is an experience that people will remember forever and hopefully pass on from generation to generation.

WOOD FOR FIRES

TINDER is the very beginning of a fire. If the proper tinder is used, a one-match fire is possible every time. Excelsior (fine curled wood shavings used for packing) is one of my favorite fire starters as it can be stored compactly and is easily obtained through many local merchants. Another excellent tinder is lint from your dryer. This is probably the most accessible fire starter for all of us. Ask a local cabinetmaker or lumber yard if they would save you their wood chips and shavings. If you decide to use material from the campsite area, please remember to use fallen twigs and sticks only. Do not disturb the beauty of our forests by cutting and disturbing living trees and bushes.

KINDLING is small, burnable material about the thickness of your thumb. It can also be pieces of split wood. A good definition for kindling is, larger than tinder but smaller than your wrist.

FUEL (FIREWOOD)   Most wood will burn easier if it is split so as to expose more cut edges to the flame. Soft wood gives off a good flame and burns fast. Soft wood works well when planning to boil or cook by reflection. Pine and cedar are good examples of soft wood. Hardwood burns longer and provides good long-lasting coals. This is excellent fuel for foil pocket cooking and flat surface cooking for bacon, eggs, pancakes, etc. Hickory, oak, birch, and maple are good long-burning hardwoods.

COOKING WITH CHARCOAL

CHARCOAL can produce a good cooking fire much faster than a wood fire. A wood fire has to be maintained continually to supply coals for cooking. Charcoal produces a uniform heat with little or no flames. This heat can be increased by fanning, or decreased by sprinkling a little water on the coals.

The safest way to begin a charcoal fire is to use a can (such as a large coffee can) that has both ends removed. Punch several holes about one-third of the way from the bottom of the can. Run pieces of a heavy gauge wire or coat hanger wire in a crisscross fashion through the holes.

To start the charcoal, place three or four stones in a circle the size of the can into the fire pit, crumple two or three sheets of newspaper and place within the stones. Place the can over the newspaper and on the lip of the stones (elevating the can on the stones will provide the needed air draft to start the charcoal), fill the upper two-thirds of the can with charcoal, and light the newspaper. In about 15 minutes, you should have red-hot coals that can be dumped into the cooking area. Keep repeating this process to assure a continual supply of coals.

Never set foil pockets, foil pots, or pans directly on the coals as the weight tends to disintegrate the coals. A single layer of coals does not provide enough heat for cooking so be sure to layer the coals. As ashes accumulate, you may need to remove them, as they will smother the fire.

When using charcoal in wet or cold weather, place the charcoal on a double thickness of heavy-weight aluminum foil. By doing this, the heat will be directed up.

FIRES FOR CAMP COOKING

TEEPEE

The teepee fire is known as the basic fire as it is the perfect beginning for all fires. Begin by placing tinder in the center of the fire pit, stacking it in the shape of a teepee. Build with the larger kindling to the outside of the tinder following the basic lines of the teepee. Next, stand the larger firewood on end, also in the form of a teepee. Make sure there is adequate air and space in and around all stages of the fire structure. Without sufficient air circulation, a good fire will not develop. The high flames of the teepee fire are especially good for reflector cooking and for boiling.

LOG CABIN

Begin the log cabin fire by stacking the tinder and kindling as is done in the teepee fire. Then, place the firewood around the teepee as if building a log cabin. The controlled flames of this fire intensifiy the heat to the center of the log cabin and coals will develop quickly. This is an excellent fire for foil pocket cooking since you can regulate how many coals are transferred to the cooking area at any given time.

CRISSCROSS

Begin the fire with the same basic teepee design. Then, lay the firewood across the fire in layers, with one layer crossing the other, making sure to leave space between the wood for air to circulate. On calm days, it may take a great deal of fanning in order to start a good fire but once it takes off, coals will develop rapidly.

FIRE PITS The best fire pit for outdoor cooking is the keyhole or double keyhole design. Most state and national campgrounds have fire rings at each campsite. These fire rings  usually have adjustable grates that perch over the slender part of the keyhole. For most cooking, start a fire in the ring and let it burn to the point that a good bed of coals starts developing. When two inches or more of coals have developed, move them under the grate and begin cooking. To regulate cooking temperatures, keep adding wood to the ring and replenish the coals as needed. The grate is usually adjustable and can be moved either away from or closer to the fire. If camping where you need to make your 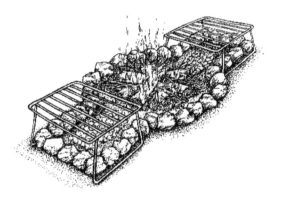 own fire pit, simply lay rocks in a keyhole or double keyhole outline. For cooking, use a portable grate over the slender part of the keyhole. The double keyhole design offers the camper two cooking areas with the main fire in the center.

BACK WOODS COOKING

Before building a fire, be sure to check the local fire regulations. In some areas, a wood campfire may not be allowed but charcoal may be used for cooking. In areas where there is a high risk of forest or prairie fires, permits for fires may be needed. When camping in a site that does not have designated fire pits, there are several precautions one must take.

- Select a spot that has at least a 15-foot diameter clearing from the nearest trees or bushes. Make sure there are no low branches hanging overhead that can be damaged by fire or actually catch on fire.

- Do not build a fire on top of a layer of peat, as the intense heat may travel downward, resulting in a peat fire.

- Be sure to clear all fallen leaves and/or pine needles within the 15-foot diameter ring.

- Place rocks in a keyhole design to contain your fire. Should you be camped in an area where there are no rocks, dig a fire trench three inches deep in a circle or keyhole shape.

- Have a shovel handy to scatter the coals and to cover them with dirt.

- If possible, have water available to help extinguish the fire.

- Always leave the campsite cleaner than you found it. It will make you feel good and I am sure the next camper will appreciate your efforts.

THE MANY USES OF FOIL

Although cooking with foil is not a new concept, let's get serious and allow aluminum foil to be the pots, pans, and bowls of your future. Cooking with foil means no heavy pots or pans to pack, carry, or wash. When foil pockets are properly sealed, you have created a miniature homemade pressure cooker. The trapped steam assures quality flavor retention. It also prevents the loss of those valuable vitamins and minerals. Exact cooking times for foil pockets are not a critical factor for turning out good-tasting meals. Sometimes it seems that the longer you have pockets over the coals, the more flavors mix and the tastier your meal becomes. Experience and experimentation will be your best teacher for cooking times.

FOIL POCKETS

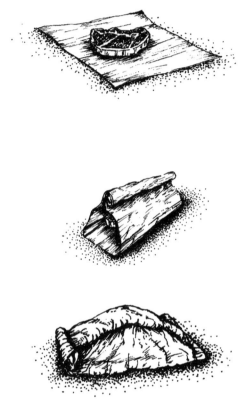

Tear off a piece of heavy-duty aluminum foil four times the circumference of the food to be sealed. Fold the foil in half, placing the food on the shiny side.

Bring the opposite sides of the foil together and fold over, one-half inch at a time, down toward the food.

The next step is to fold the open edges toward the center, crimping to form an airtight seal. If steam is allowed to escape, food may scorch.

WARNING: Open foil pockets carefully, away from the fire. Pockets will be very hot and escaping steam may cause burns.

FOIL POTS

For strength, mold four layers of heavy-duty aluminum foil over an inverted plastic container or can of desired size.

Roll the edges to give added strength. A lid can be made by simply laying a piece of foil over the pot and turning the edges under the rolled rim.

FOIL BOWLS   Prepare the bowls the same way as you would the pots, but use only two thickness of heavy-duty foil.

FOIL PAN AND/OR SKILLET

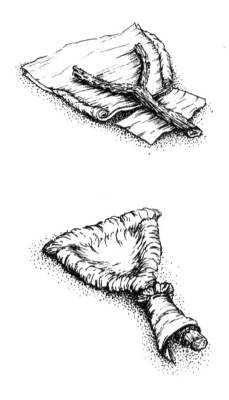

Tear off a piece of heavy-duty aluminum foil four times the width of a forked stick that has a Y about 12 inches wide at the top. The handle part of the stick should be about 12 to 14 inches long.

Fold the foil over the forked portion of the stick. Roll the foil toward the forks and crimp around each tine.

Roll the top edge down to form a triangle. After turning it over, gently push on the center to create an indented cooking area.

FOIL SKILLET

A camp skillet can be made with an ordinary coat hanger. Grip the bottom of the hanger in the middle and pull downward into a diamond shape. Curl the hook around a stick to form a handle.

Tear off a sheet of heavy-duty aluminum foil four times the width of the hanger. Fold the foil in thirds and lay across the hanger. Begin rolling the foil toward the wire form, crimping it around the metal.

As with the forked stick, turn the hanger over and gently push on the center to indent it for cooking.

DRIP-O-LATOR COFFEE
OR TEA POT

Form the coffee or tea pot bottom by placing two thicknesses of heavy-duty aluminum foil over an inverted 1-pound coffee can. Remove the can and roll the edges. Make the top of the pot the same way, only slightly smaller.

Prick the bottom of the top part several times with a pin or needle and line it with a paper towel. The towel will serve as a coffee or tea filter.

Place desired amount of coffee or tea in the top part and set on top of the bottom container. Pour boiling water over the coffee or tea and when the water has drained through to the bottom container, you are ready to enjoy a delicious cup of your favorite camp beverage.

REFLECTOR OVEN

To make a reflector oven from aluminum foil, you will need the following sticks:

> 2 straight sticks 24 to 26 inches in length with a 2-inch fork on one end
>
> 4 straight sticks 3 inches in length with a 2-inch fork on one end
>
> 3 straight sticks 22 to 23 inches in length

Place the two long, forked sticks into the ground at the edge of the fire pit approximately 19 inches apart. Wrap heavy-duty aluminum foil (18-inch width, shiny side in) around a straight stick, crimping to make it secure, and place across the two forked sticks already in the ground. Unroll the foil toward the ground at a 45° **angle**. At ground level, place another straight stick to the inside of the foil and secure ends by inverting two of the 3-inch forked sticks into the ground.

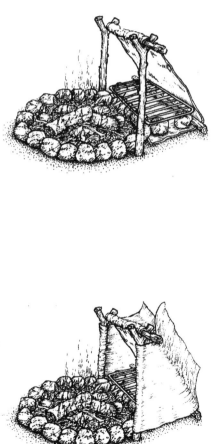

Bring the remaining foil forward along the ground to the edge of the fire and roll the edge around the remaining straight stick and secure with the final two 3-inch forked sticks.

To complete the oven, wrap foil around each of the standing forked sticks and unroll foil toward the center back of the oven. Secure the two pieces together by making three $1/2$-inch folds or until there is no longer any slack in the foil. To inspect food within the oven, unfold one side panel from the back.

OUTDOOR MEAL PLANNING

Forget the boxed doughnuts, candy, and all other junk food. Let's take some pride in what can be prepared, with ease, on a camping trip. You will find that your confidence will build to new heights as you experiment with *Foil Cookery*. Your friends and relatives will be amazed at the wonderful foods that can be created over the campfire.

FOUR BASIC FOOD GROUPS

DAIRY FOOD GROUP
Group includes: milk, yogurt, ice cream, cheese, and butter
Recommended Servings
Adults: 2 servings daily
Children: 3 - 4 servings daily

MEAT FOOD GROUP
Group includes: meat, fish, poultry, dried peas, beans, eggs, and lentils
Recommended Servings
Adults and Children: 2 - 3 servings daily

VEGETABLE AND FRUIT GROUP
Recommended Servings
Adults and Children:
Leafy green and yellow vegetables - 1 serving daily

Citrus fruits and tomatoes - 1 serving daily

Other vegetables and fruits - 2 or more servings daily

BREAD AND CEREAL GROUP
Group includes - breads, cereals, hot or cold rice, and pasta

Recommended Servings
Adults and Children: 5 servings daily

SUGGESTED BREAKFAST FARE

Keep in mind that these are only samples. Add your own ideas that suit your tastes and the tastes of those camping with you. Pancakes with applesauce or my favorite, apple butter, bacon or sausage and milk is a hearty, hard-to-pass-up breakfast in the open air.

FRUITS, RAW
Pears, grapefruits, bananas, strawberries, apples, raspberries, oranges, blueberries, peaches, blackberries, melons, tangerines, grapes, nectarines, plums, or pineapple

FRUITS, DRIED
Apples, prunes, apricots, raisins, bananas, pineapple, and/or trail mixes

FRUITS, CANNED

Applesauce, peaches, pears, pineapple, fruit cocktail, or apricots

EGGS

Scrambled, basted, fried, boiled, poached, omelet, or baked

MEATS

Bacon, sausage, ham, hamburger, or steaks

VEGETABLES

Fried potatoes or potato cakes

CEREALS

Hot or cold served with fruit or juice and milk

LUNCH

—as light or as hearty as you choose

Many times, when we are camping, lunch is a light, non-cooked type meal. That way, if we want to hike, fish, shop for antiques in local towns, or just relax, we aren't dependent upon a fire for lunch. Sandwiches are generally the standard fare. Sometimes we prepare them ahead of time so we can take them with us, or sometimes we put a quick lunch together at the campsite. There is nothing more nutritious than a freshly made sandwich, piled high with the condiments of choice, fresh sliced tomatoes and onions, fresh or dried fruits, and a beverage.

DINNER

Okay, food fanciers, this is the time of day to let out all the stops, let your imagination run wild - prove to your loved ones that you can cook as well over an open fire as you can in your own home with all the food processors, microwaves, utensils, temperature controls, pots, pans, and just plain gadgets that are neat, but what do they do?

PROTECTING
THE ENVIRONMENT

As we go on our great weekend and vacation camping adventures, we must make a pact with ourselves to protect the natural order of the environment. We must be observers of nature, taking care not to destroy the very beauty that can be ours forever.

As an observer, notice the many varieties of trees, shrubs, plants, etc. that are within eyesight. Nature has provided a safety valve. For example, if one variety of tree becomes diseased and the entire area is void of that species, the other trees will mature and fill in the forest. The dead trees will slowly decay and provide rich nutrients for other species of trees to fully develop. If left alone, nature can take care of herself. We must be careful not to interfere with her timing.

As citizens, we share the responsibility of being caretaker of this great land of ours. The best camping conservation program to adopt is one that is least harmful to the environment.

- Carry trash bags and use them.
- Camp in designated areas only.
- Do not cut down trees or break off branches to use as fire-wood.
- Never leave a fire unattended.
- Always make sure the fire is completely extinguished by dousing with water or dirt and scattering the ashes.

- Know what can be recycled and do it.
- Do not burn garbage, paper, plastic, or metal.
- Use available restroom facilities. If in the wilderness, dig catholes and then replace the dirt and sod. Carry paper products out with you by placing in a plastic bag.
- Do not clean fish, dishes, or clothing, or bathe in streams or lakes.
- Make sure soap products do not make their way into waterways.
- Properly dispose of, or store, leftovers and grease after each meal.
- Do not feed the wildlife, as it encourages them to depend upon humans for food. They may be cute, but they can also be dangerous.
- Make sure your campsite is not a source for noise pollution.
- When hiking, stay on the trails.

Campgrounds and wilderness areas are treasures that, if used wisely, will provide pleasure for future generations. Subtle changes are constantly taking place in nature and it is our privilege to observe these changes, not alter them. We are, after all, only visitors and we should preserve what is ours to enjoy.

Table of Measurements & Substitutions

Standard Measurements

tsp (teaspoon), Tbsp (tablespoon)

oz (ounce), qt (quart)

Pinch .... $^1/_8$ tsp

3 tsp .... 1 Tbsp

2 Tbsp .... $^1/_8$ cup

4 Tbsp .... $^1/_4$ cup

5 Tbsp + 1 tsp . $^1/_3$ cup

8 Tbsp .... $^1/_2$ cup

10 Tbsp + 2 tsp $^2/_3$ cup

12 Tbsp .... $^3/_4$ cup

16 Tbsp .... 1 cup

2 Tbsp ...1 liquid ounce

4 oz .... $^1/_2$ cup

8 oz .... 1 cup

2 cups .... 1 pint

2 pints .... 1 quart

1qt ....4 cups

4 qts .... 1 gallon

8qts .... 1 peck

4 pecks ....1 bushel

16 oz (dry measure) 1 lb

1 liter .... 33.8 oz

Table of Substitutions & Equivalents

1 cup fine crumbs	22 vanilla wafers
	4 slices of bread
	26 saltine crackers
	14 graham crackers
1 cup whole milk	$1/2$ cup evaporated milk + $1/2$ cup water
1 Tbsp instant minced onion	1 small fresh onion
1 Tbsp prepared mustard	1 tsp dry mustard
1 cup sugar	$2/3$ to $3/4$ cup honey
	$1 1/2$ cups maple syrup + $1/4$ tsp bk soda
1 whole egg	2 egg whites
	$1/4$ cup egg substitute
1 cup sour cream	1 cup plain, low-fat yogurt
1 oz baking chocolate	3 Tbsp cocoa powder + 1 Tbsp oil
1 Tbsp fresh herbs	1 tsp dry herbs
1 Tbsp cornstarch (for thickening)	2 Tbsp flour
1 cup sour milk	1 cup sweet milk + 1 Tbsp lemon juice
1 lb apples	3 medium apples (3 cups sliced)
$1/2$ lb cheddar cheese	2 cups grated cheese
1 lb potatoes	3 medium potatoes ($2 1/3$ cup sliced)

Breakfasts

Apples and Raisins

They will want seconds —
be sure to make plenty!

4 tart apples, cored and quartered
$^1/_2$ cup raisins
$^3/_4$ cup brown sugar
2 Tbsp margarine

Place all ingredients on a double thickness of heavy duty aluminum foil. Seal the foil pocket and place on a grate over hot coals. Cook 20 minutes or until apples are tender. Serve with biscuits or buttered toast. Serves 4.

Applesauce and Granola with Dumplings

Something for that
morning sweet tooth!

2 cans (15.5 oz) applesauce
1 tsp cinnamon
$^1/_2$ cup granola
2 cups biscuit mix
$^2/_3$ cup milk

Bring applesauce to a simmer in a foil pot on a grate over hot coals. Sprinkle cinnamon and granola on top.

In a foil bowl, stir milk into the biscuit mix. Drop dumplings by spoonfuls into the applesauce mixture. Cook covered for 10 minutes and 10 minutes uncovered. Serves 4-6.

Aunt's Pancakes

I have many fond memories of going to my aunt and uncle's house when I was a kid. One memory is waking up on Saturday morning to the wonderful aroma of these pancakes.

3 cups flour
3 tsp baking powder
3 tsp baking soda
3 eggs
1 quart buttermilk
$^{3}/_{4}$ tsp salt

Combine dry ingredients in a foil bowl. Add eggs and buttermilk. Stir until batter is mostly smooth—there may be a few lumps.

Cook on 4 thicknesses of oiled aluminum foil on a grate over medium hot coals or in a reflector oven. Serves 8 - 10.

Bacon and Eggs Plus

Cream-style corn adds a burst of flavor
to this old-fashioned breakfast

4 slices bacon, cut up
1 can (14.75 oz) cream-style corn
8 eggs, lightly beaten
Salt and pepper, to taste

Place a foil skillet on a grate over medium-hot coals. Fry bacon until crisp; drain off grease. Add corn; simmer until heated through, stirring occasionally.

Add eggs, season with salt and pepper, and scramble until eggs are done and no longer shiny. Serve immediately. Serves 4.

Breakfast Muffin

3 English muffins
6 eggs
$\frac{1}{4}$ cup sliced green onions
$\frac{1}{2}$ red pepper, diced
2 Tbsp margarine
Salt and pepper to taste
$\frac{3}{4}$ cup chunky salsa
12 strips cheddar cheese

Beat eggs, onions, pepper, and salt and pepper in a foil bowl. Melt margarine in a foil pan on a grate over medium-hot coals. Add egg mixture, stirring until eggs are cooked.

Place muffin halves on a sheet of heavy duty aluminum foil. Spoon eggs onto muffin halves, then cover with salsa and cheese. Seal foil pocket, place on a grate over coals for about 10 minutes, or until cheese is melted. Serves 3 - 6.

Campfire Steak and Eggs
This will start your day off right

4 breakfast steaks, cubed
4-8 eggs *
2 Tbsp margarine
Salt and pepper to taste

Melt margarine in a foil skillet over medium hot coals. Add meat, stirring to brown on both sides. Add eggs, salt, and pepper. Stir until eggs are done. Serves 4.

* Use 4 eggs for a lighter breakfast — 8 for heartier appetites.

Cheesy Sausage Biscuits

1 lb ground sausage
1 can (17.3 oz) large refrigerator biscuits (8 count)
4 slices cheese

Make four sausage patties. Cook in a foil skillet on a grate over hot coals until done. Roll biscuits to $\frac{1}{8}$-inch thickness. Arrange sausage patties and cheese on four of the biscuits. Top with remaining biscuits and seal edges with a fork. Brush each side with vegetable oil and place on double thickness of heavy duty aluminum foil. Seal pockets loosely, giving biscuits room to raise. Place on a grate over hot coals. Bake 10 minutes per side, or until biscuits are done. If you prefer, try baking these in your foil reflector oven, turning to bake all sides evenly. Serves 4.

Cheesy Scramble
Turns plain eggs
into something special!

8 eggs
Processed cheese, 1-inch thick, cubed
4 slices toast, cubed
4 Tbsp margarine

Melt 2 Tbsp margarine in a foil pan over medium-hot coals. Add toast cubes and toss until coated; set aside.

Melt remaining margarine, then add eggs and cheese, stirring to scramble. Cook until eggs are done and cheese is melted. Serve with toast cubes scattered over top of eggs. Serves 4.

Corned Beef Hash and Eggs

Your own personal egg cup plus!
This is fun to prepare.

2 cans (15 oz. each) corned beef hash
4 eggs
Salt and pepper, to taste

Wrap a double thickness of heavy duty aluminum foil around the hash cans, forming cups. Make a total of 4 cups. Carefully remove foil and roll edges. Divide hash into each foil cup, leaving a dent or well in the center of the hash.

Place filled cups on a grate over hot coals. When hash is hot and bubbly, crack an egg into the center of each cup. Salt and pepper to taste. Cover, and allow eggs to cook to desired doneness. Serves 4.

Cream of Wheat and Syrup

Cream of Wheat cereal
Maple or other flavored syrup

Prepare Cream of Wheat according to package directions in a foil pot on a grate over hot coals. Pour cereal into a foil cylinder; chill thoroughly. Carefully remove foil and slice Cream of Wheat into $1/2$-inch thick pieces.

Fry in a small amount of margarine in a foil pan on a grate over hot coals, turning until both sides are brown and crispy. Serve with your favorite syrup.

Eggs A-La-Camp
You can eat like a king . . .
even in the woods.

8 eggs
3 cups milk
7 Tbsp flour
1 stick margarine
Salt and pepper, to taste

Set a foil pot on a grate over hot coals. Place eggs in the pot and cover with salted water. Hard boil eggs for at least 10 minutes.

Meanwhile, melt margarine in another foil pot. Add flour, stirring until smooth. Slowly pour in milk, stirring until mixture is thickened. Salt and pepper to taste.

Peel cooked eggs and chop, reserving 2 yolks. Add chopped eggs to white sauce, stirring to mix. Serve over toast or biscuits. Grate reserved yolks over mixture. Serves 4-6.

Gravy and Biscuits
As American as apple pie

1 lb sausage
7 Tbsp flour
3 cups milk
1 can large refrigerator biscuits (8 count)
Salt and pepper, to taste

Bake biscuits in a reflector oven on oiled foil, turning to bake all sides.

Place sausage in a foil pot on a grate over hot coals. Cook, stirring to crumble, until sausage is well browned and done. Drain off grease.

Add flour, milk, salt, and pepper, stirring until thickened. Serve over biscuits. Serves 4.

Make Any Cold Cereal . . . HOT

I can remember my mother fixing my dad shredded wheat this way as I was growing up. It is not only good, but it helps take the edge off a cool morning. It's also a quick and easy breakfast for hunters and fishermen!

4 servings favorite cold cereal
2 cups hot water

Pour hot water over the cold cereal to soften, then drain the water. Cover with milk and desired fruit. Serves 4.

Mashed Potato Cakes and Eggs

Always a camp favorite

4 medium potatoes, pared and diced
$1/4$ cup milk
4-8 eggs (1-2 eggs per person)
Salt and pepper, to taste

Boil potatoes in a foil pot on a grate over hot coals until tender; drain. Mash potatoes, adding milk to make a smooth consistency. Salt and pepper to taste. Set aside to cool.

Make patties and coat with flour. Cook in small amount of margarine in a foil skillet on a grate over hot coals. In another foil skillet, fry eggs in small amount of margarine to desired doneness. Serve together along with toast. Serves 4-8.

Orange Fry Bread
Good morning sunshine!!

3 eggs
1 cup orange juice
1 Tbsp sugar
$^1/_4$ tsp salt
$^1/_4$ cup margarine
1 tsp ground cinnamon
8 slices white bread

Beat first 4 ingredients until well mixed. Melt half the margarine in a foil skillet on a grate over medium   hot coals. Dip 4 slices of bread in the egg mixture and fry until golden brown. Repeat this process for the remaining 4 slices of bread.

*Sprinkle lightly with cinnamon before serving. Serves 4.

*Also good with a light spread of orange marmalade.

Poor Man's Breakfast
Rich man or poor man —try it, it's good.

4 slices bologna, edges scored
4 eggs
8 slices toast
3 Tbsp margarine
Salt and pepper, to taste

Melt margarine in a foil pan over medium hot coals. Add bologna slices and fry until browned. Crack an egg over each slice of bologna. Fry for 5 minutes, then turn. Continue cooking until done. Serve on toast or bread. Serves 4.

Potato/Egg Casserole

Even my friend who hates eggs
enjoys this on a cold morning.

2 potatoes, pared and diced
3 Tbsp vegetable oil
$^1/_4$ cup green onions, sliced
8 eggs
2 Tbsp parmesan cheese
Salt and pepper to taste

Heat oil in a foil pan on a grate over medium hot coals. Add potatoes
and fry until browned and tender. Add eggs and onions, stirring to
scramble. Continue cooking until eggs are done. Serve with parmesan
cheese sprinkled on top. Serves 4.

Scrambler Biscuits

Really rise and shine with these!

1 pkg (5 count) large buttermilk biscuits
5 slices bacon
10 eggs
4 slices Mexican-flavored cheese
2 Tbsp butter or margarine
Salt and pepper, to taste
5 pre-formed aluminum cupcake tins

Open biscuit package and separate biscuits. Roll out each biscuit to
4½" diameter.

Spray outside surfaces of cupcake tins with nonstick cooking
spray. Shape dough around the outside of the tins. Place upside

down in a heated reflector oven and bake for 10-12 minutes, or until golden brown. If you don't have a reflector oven, arrange formed biscuits upside down on a piece of heavy duty aluminum foil. Place on a grate over medium-hot coals; cover with a loosely-fitting aluminum foil tent and bake for 10 minutes, or until golden brown.

Carefully remove tins from biscuits. Set biscuit cups aside and keep warm.

Meanwhile, cook bacon in a foil skillet on a grate placed over hot coals until done. Drain bacon on paper toweling, then crumble.

Melt margarine in a foil pan; add eggs, salt, and pepper. Stir to scramble. Add cheese and continue stirring until cheese is melted.

Spoon eggs evenly into biscuit cups. Sprinkle with crumbled bacon and serve. Serves 5.

South of the Border Eggs

Thank you, Mexico.
We like this up north too.

8 eggs
$1/4$ cup green onions, sliced
8 slices bacon, crumbled
Salt and pepper, to taste
8 flour tortillas (20-oz burrito size)
Favorite chunky salsa

Fry bacon in foil skillet on grate over hot coals. When done, drain on paper towels and crumble. Scramble eggs, green onions, salt and pepper until done in foil pan on grate over hot coals. Stir in bacon. Place egg mixture down the center of the tortillas. Cover with desired amount of salsa, roll and enjoy. Serves 4.

Strictly Southern

It may be southern, but don't let
that stop you northerners!

2 cans (14.5 oz) yellow hominy, drained
4 slices bacon, crumbled
8 eggs
4 Tbsp margarine
Salt and pepper, to taste

Fry bacon in a foil pan on a grate over medium hot coals; drain. When bacon has cooled, crumble and set aside.

Melt 2 Tbsp margarine in a foil skillet. Add hominy, fry until well heated, then remove to 4 serving plates.

Melt remaining margarine in the skillet. Fry eggs to desired doneness. Serve with bacon scattered on hominy and eggs on the side. Serves 4.

Western Scramble

When ready to serve, drizzle some melted cheese on top,
and maybe even some salsa.

8 eggs
3 Tbsp green onions, sliced
1 Tbsp pimentos, chopped
1 Tbsp margarine
Salt and pepper, to taste

Whip eggs in an aluminum foil bowl until well mixed. Add onions, pimentos, salt, and pepper. Meanwhile, melt margarine in a foil pan on a grate placed over medium-hot coals. Add egg mixture and stir until eggs are firm. Serves 4.

Salads

Banana Nut Salad

A quick and easy salad, with a
taste your family will love.

4 bananas, peeled
$^2/_3$ cup salad dressing
$^2/_3$ cup finely chopped nuts

Roll whole bananas in salad dressing and then in chopped nuts, coating
well. Chill in the cooler until ready to serve. Serves 4.

Note: Bananas should be ripe, but not overly so. Save over ripe bananas
for banana nut bread.

BLT Garden Salad

My husband likes to add pineapple chunks,
grapes, and fresh sliced peaches.

8 slices bacon
1 16-oz pkg salad greens
1 large or 2 small tomatoes, cut into $^1/_2$" pieces
3 green onions, chopped
1 small cucumber, diced
5 red radishes, thinly sliced
1 large carrot, grated
$^1/_2$ cup light ranch dressing

Place a foil skillet on a grate over medium-hot coals. Cut uncooked
bacon into 1-inch pieces and fry until crisp. Drain bacon on paper towels.
Toss bacon pieces with remaining ingredients and serve immediately.
Serves 4.

Carrot Salad
The perfect summer salad

10 carrots, pared and grated
$^1/_4$ cup raisins
$^1/_4$ cup salad dressing

Combine all ingredients in a foil bowl and place in the cooler until ready to serve. Serves 4.

Carrot-Apple Salad

6 carrots, grated
1 tart apple, cored and diced
2 Tbsp raisins
$^1/_4$ cup low-fat yogurt
3 Tbsp skim milk
2 tsp sugar or sugar substitute equivalent
$^1/_4$ tsp ground nutmeg
$^1/_4$ tsp ground cinnamon

Combine all ingredients in a foil bowl and mix thoroughly. Cover salad and chill in the cooler until ready to serve. Serves 4.

Cool Cucumber Salad
As cool as it gets!

4 cucumbers, sliced
1 bottle blended Italian dressing

Cover cucumber slices with dressing. Chill in the cooler until ready to serve. Serves 4-6.

Cottage Peach Salad

A pretty, as well as tasty, salad to serve on hot summer days

1 12-oz container small curd cottage cheese
$\frac{1}{2}$ cup raisins
$\frac{1}{4}$ cup English walnuts, chopped
1 8.5-oz can sliced peaches, drained
4 lettuce leaves

Blend cottage cheese, raisins, and walnuts in a foil bowl. Divide mixture onto lettuce leaves and garnish with peach slices. If desired, top with 1 tsp mayonnaise or salad dressing. Serves 4.

Dad's Wilted Lettuce

Sowing of lettuce seeds was a spring ritual for my dad. It was fun watching him caring for it as he eagerly anticipated the first harvest.

Fresh garden lettuce, torn
3 slices bacon, crumbled
2 Tbsp bacon drippings

Fry bacon in a foil skillet on a grate over medium hot coals. Reserve bacon drippings.

Crumble bacon over lettuce and dribble on hot bacon drippings. Serve warm. Serves 2.

Easy Fruit Salad

A favorite at family picnics and summer pot luck dinners

1 can fruit cocktail, drained
1 banana, sliced
1 tart apple, cored and diced
$^1/_4$ cup chopped nuts
$^1/_3$ cup salad dressing

Mix all ingredients in a foil bowl. Chill until ready to serve. Serves 4.

Note: If you prefer all fresh fruit, simply substitute fresh peaches, pears, seedless grapes, and maraschino cherries for the canned fruit cocktail.

Eye-Catching Stuffed Lettuce

1 head lettuce
1 3-oz pkg cream cheese
2 Tbsp roquefort cheese
2 Tbsp carrots, grated
2 Tbsp tomato, seeded
1 Tbsp green pepper, minced
1 Tbsp onion, minced
Dash salt and pepper

Wash lettuce. Remove any bad outer leaves. Remove core, leaving a hole 2 inches in diameter.

Combine cheeses, blending thoroughly. Add remaining ingredients in order given; mix well. Fill hollow in lettuce with mixture, packing in firmly. Wrap lettuce in aluminum foil and chill in cooler until center is firm.

To serve, cut lettuce head in crosswise slices. Serves 4-6.

French Rice Salad

1 cup cooked rice

$^{1}/_{2}$ yellow pepper, diced

3 green onions, sliced

1 stalk celery, thinly sliced

$^{1}/_{4}$ cup carrots, grated

1 tomato, seeded and chopped

$^{1}/_{4}$ cup lite French salad dressing

Mix rice and dressing in a foil bowl. Add vegetables. Toss to mix. Cover and place in a cooler until ready to serve. Serves 4.

Variation: Rice is a good base to start with. Top with any dressing of your choice and any combination of vegetables.

Healthy Vegetable Salad

Yogurt reduces the fat and calories in this creamy vegetable salad

$^{1}/_{2}$ cup plain low-fat yogurt

2 Tbsp red wine vinegar

1 Tbsp virgin olive oil

Salt and pepper, to taste

$^{1}/_{2}$ cup broccoli florets

$^{1}/_{2}$ red pepper, seeded and diced

2 carrots, thinly sliced

1 tomato, seeded and chopped

$^{1}/_{4}$ cup green onions, thinly sliced

Combine yogurt, vinegar and oil in a foil bowl. Add salt and pepper to taste; mix well and set aside.

Add broccoli, red pepper, carrots, tomato, and onions. Pour yogurt dressing over vegetables; toss to coat well. Cover salad and place in cooler until ready to serve. Serves 4.

Indian Summer Salad
Autumn ripe fruits and vegetables combine
to make a flavorful and colorful salad

Juice from 1 orange
1 tsp orange zest
3 Tbsp apple juice
1 Tbsp olive oil
1 Tbsp fresh mint, chopped
4 small sweet potatoes, cooked, peeled and cubed
1 tart apple, diced
$\frac{1}{2}$ cup celery, diced
$\frac{1}{3}$ cup pecans, chopped
$\frac{1}{4}$ cup raisins

Combine orange juice, orange zest, apple juice, olive oil, and mint in an aluminum foil bowl. Add sweet potatoes, apple, pecans, and raisins. Toss to evenly coat. Serve immediately or chill in cooler until ready to serve. Serves 4.

Peanut Butter Salad

4 tart apples, diced
1 stalk celery, thinly sliced
$\frac{1}{4}$ cup raisins
$\frac{1}{2}$ cup chunky peanut butter
3 Tbsp salad dressing

Combine all ingredients in a foil bowl, seal, and chill in the cooler. Serves 6.

Pear Nut Salad

1 can (15.25-oz) sliced pears
$1/4$ cup salad dressing
$1/3$ cup chopped nuts

Lightly toss pears in salad dressing and top with nuts. Chill in the cooler until ready to serve. Serves 4.

Potato - Bacon Salad

Takes the ordinary out of this summer favorite

4 potatoes, boiled
6 slices bacon, crumbled
$1/2$ cucumber, diced
4 green onions, sliced
$1/4$ cup mayonnaise
Salt and pepper to taste

Boil potatoes in a foil pot on a grate over hot coals until fork-tender. When cool, peel and cube potatoes.

Meanwhile, fry bacon in a foil skillet on a grate over hot coals, drain on paper towels and crumble. Combine all ingredients in a foil bowl and chill in the cooler to allow flavors to mix. Serves 4-6.

Rancho Salsa Pollo Salad
Nice light meal for a hot day

2 boneless, skinless chicken breasts, cut into strips
$^1/_2$ cup thick and chunky salsa
1 16-oz pkg salad greens
$^1/_2$ cup shredded cheddar cheese

Dressing:
$^1/_2$ cup thick and chunky salsa
$^1/_2$ cup light ranch dressing

Place an aluminum foil skillet on a grate over hot coals. Add chicken strips and salsa until chicken is cooked through and no longer pink. Remove from fire and set aside to cool.

Combine chicken, salad greens, and cheese in a large bowl; toss lightly. Top with dressing and serve. Serves 4.

Sliced Lettuce Salad
Talk about easy! The sunflower
seeds add a nutty crunch and
transform a simple lettuce salad
into something special.

1 head lettuce, cut into
$^1/_2$-inch slices
2 carrots, grated
Favorite salad dressing
$^1/_3$ cup hulled sunflower seeds

Arrange lettuce slices on plates, top with dressing, and finally, sprinkle on carrots and sunflower seeds. Serves 6.

South Texas Salad

Try it . . .Texas can't keep this one!

1 can (15 oz) red beans, drained
$^1/_2$ cup green onions, sliced
3 slices bacon, crumbled
$^1/_4$ green pepper, diced
$^1/_4$ yellow pepper, diced
1 cucumber, diced
1 tomato, deseeded and diced
$^1/_2$ cup favorite salsa

Fry bacon in a foil skillet on a grate over medium hot coals. Drain on paper towels, crumble, and set aside. Combine remaining ingredients in a foil bowl. Chill in the cooler until ready to serve. Sprinkle with crumbled bacon pieces before serving. Serves 4-6.

Tuna Salad

1 can ($6^1/_2$ oz) tuna, drained
$^1/_4$ cup mayonnaise
$^1/_4$ cup pickle relish
$^1/_4$ cup chopped celery
3 green onions, sliced

Mix all ingredients in a foil bowl. Store in the cooler. Serve with tomato wedges and toast tips. Serves 4.

Vegetable Medley Salad

Every mom will be proud to serve this one.

2 cucumbers, thinly sliced
2 tomatoes, diced, seeds removed
4 green onions, sliced
1 stalk celery, thinly sliced
2 carrots, shredded
1 cup broccoli florets
1 cup cauliflower florets
1 small bottle favorite salad dressing

Blend dressing with vegetables, cover, and set in the cooler until ready to serve. Serves 4-6.

White & Green Floret Salad

$1^1/_2$ cups cauliflower florets
$1^1/_2$ cups broccoli florets
$^1/_2$ cup green onions, sliced
$^3/_4$ cup Italian dressing

Mix ingredients in a foil bowl and chill in the cooler until ready to serve. Top with croutons, if desired. Serves 4-6.

Sandwiches

Cheese & Onion Enchiladas

1 pkg flour tortillas, taco size
2 cups cheddar cheese, grated
1 cup onions, minced
1 small jar thick and chunky picante sauce
$^1/_2$ large box soft processed cheese

Heat processed cheese and picante sauce in a foil pan on a grate over medium-hot coals, stirring until cheese is melted. Place cheddar cheese and onions in the center of each tortilla. Roll and tuck ends.

Place rolled tortillas on a double thickness of heavy duty aluminum foil. Cover with cheese/sauce mixture and loosely seal pocket.

Heat on a grate over medium hot coals for 10 minutes. Serves 4-6.

Cheesy Italian Sloppy Joes

1 lb ground chuck
1 medium onion, diced
$^3/_4$ cup chunky spaghetti sauce
4 slices mozzarella cheese, halved
4 kaiser buns

Brown hamburger and onion, stirring to crumble, in a foil skillet on a grate over hot coals. Drain grease, add spaghetti sauce; simmer 15 minutes.

Cut buns in half and place one-half slice of cheese on the bottom half. Divide the hamburger mixture among the buns. Top with remaining slices of cheese and bun tops.

Place on a double thickness of heavy duty aluminum foil and seal. Heat on a grate over hot coals until cheese is melted, about 10 minutes. Serves 4.

Chicken Sandwich Spread
Perfect on-the-go lunch

2 cans (5 oz each) breast of chicken (packed in water),
    drained
1 tart apple, diced
2 green onions, thinly sliced
1 Tbsp unsalted dry roasted peanuts, chopped
3 Tbsp non-fat mayonnaise

Combine all ingredients in a foil bowl, stirring until well mixed. Serve
as a spread on whole grain bread or multi-grain crackers.
Serves 4-6.

Double Covered Dogs
Not just for kids

1 package jumbo hot dogs   (8 count)
8 slices bacon
4 slices cheese

Heat a foil skillet on a grate over medium-hot coals. Spiral wrap each
hot dog with one strip of bacon. Fry in the skillet until bacon is crisp;
drain off grease. Cover hot dogs with cheese and continue cooking until
cheese is melted. Serve on hot dog buns. Serves 4 - 8.

Easy Bar-be-que Chicken on Bun

4 cans (5 oz each) chunk white chicken
1 red pepper, sliced into rings
$^3/_4$ cup favorite barbeque sauce
1 cup shreaded mozzarella cheese
8 onion buns

Heat chicken and barbeque sauce in a foil pot on a grate over medium hot coals. Divide mixture between buns. Top with pepper rings, cheese, and the top half of buns.

Place on a double thickness of heavy duty aluminum foil and seal. Heat on a grate over hot coals until cheese is melted, about 10 minutes. Serves 8.

English Muffin Pizzas

8 English muffins, halved
$^3/_4$ cup pizza sauce
$^3/_4$ cup pepperoni, diced
1 cup mozzarella cheese

Spread each muffin half with pizza sauce, sprinkle on pepperoni, and cover with cheese. Place in a foil reflector oven and heat until cheese is melted. Serves 4 - 8.

French Turkey Bake

$^1/_2$ lb deli turkey meat, thinly sliced
4 hard boiled eggs, chopped
4 green onions, sliced
$^1/_4$ cup poppy seed salad dressing
$^3/_4$ cup cheddar cheese, shredded
1 loaf French bread, halved lengthwise

Place eggs in foil pot of boiling water on grate over hot flames. Boil hard for 15 minutes. Plunge cooked eggs into cold water. When cool, peel eggs and chop.

Combine eggs, green onions and salad dressing in a foil bowl; mix well.

Meanwhile, cut French bread lengthwise. Arrange turkey evenly on bread halves. Spread egg mixture over turkey and sprinkle with cheese. Heat in reflector oven 10-12 minutes or until cheese is melted. Serves 4-6.

Grilled Pastrami Sandwich

8 slices rye bread
16 slices pastrami
1 med red onion, sliced thin
1 stalk celery, thinly sliced
4 Tbsp Italian dressing
4 slices cheddar cheese
3 Tbsp margarine

Sauté onions and celery in Italian dressing in a foil pan on a grate over medium-hot coals. Meanwhile, butter one side of each slice of bread.

Place four slices of bread, butter side down, in a second foil skillet on a grate over medium-hot coals. Place one-fourth of the onion-celery mixture on each slice of bread. Top with pastrami, cheese, and remaining four slices of bread. Grill until both sides are golden brown and cheese is melted. Serves 4.

Hamburger/Onion Joes

Need a quick lunch? Try these.

1 lb ground chuck
1 can (10.5-oz) onion soup
$^1/_4$ tsp pepper
1 - 2 Tbsp flour

Season hamburger with pepper. Brown in a foil pan on a grate over hot coals, stirring to crumble; drain off grease. Add soup and flour; stir until heated through and thickened. Serve over buns or biscuits and eat with a fork. Serves 4 - 6.

Hot Italian Subs

Quick to assemble

$^1/_2$ loaf Italian bread, sliced lengthwise
8 slices mozzarella cheese
8 slices pastrami, thinly sliced
1 tomato, thinly sliced
1 onion, thinly sliced
2 Tbsp black olives, sliced
$^1/_8$ tsp pepper
Italian dressing to taste

Scoop some of the bread out of the lower half, leaving it about $^1/_2$" thick. Layer half the cheese, and all the pastrami and tomatoes in the shell. Top with onion slices, black olives, pepper, and salad dressing. Layer on remaining cheese.

Place in reflector oven and cook until cheese has melted. Top with remaining bread half and slice into 4 sections. Serve immediately. Serves 4.

More Than a Burger - Bacon, Egg & Cheese

$1^1/_2$ lbs ground chuck
8 slices bacon
4 eggs
Salt and pepper to taste
4 hamburger buns
4 slices cheddar cheese
Mayonnaise, to taste

Make four hamburger patties. Cover a grate with heavy duty aluminum foil. Cook hamburger over medium hot coals until well done. Season to taste.

Fry bacon over medium hot coals until brown and crisp. Drain on paper towels. Fry eggs in bacon grease until hard cooked. Drain on paper towels.

Place all ingredients on each bun. Top with cheddar cheese and mayonnaise. Serves 4.

Not Just a Burger - German
A taste of the Old World —
tangy goodness

2 lbs ground chuck
1 can sauerkraut, drained

Make eight thin hamburger patties. Divide sauerkraut onto four of the patties. Cover with remaining four hamburger patties, sealing well.

Place on a double thickness of heavy duty aluminum foil. Salt and pepper to taste. Seal pockets tightly and place on a grate over hot coals.

Cook for 15 to 20 minutes, then turn pockets over. Continue cooking for an additional 15 to 20 minutes. Serves 4.

More Than a Burger - Peanut Butter

Don't turn your nose up at this combination.
Once you've tried it, you'll want it again and again.

1$^1/_2$ lbs ground chuck
4 Tbsp peanut butter
4 tomato slices
4 sweet onion slices
4 lettuce leaves
Mayonnaise or salad dressing, to taste
Salt and pepper, to taste
4 hamburger buns

Make four hamburger patties. Cover a grate with heavy duty aluminum foil. Cook hamburger over medium hot coals until well done. Season to taste.

When done, add remaining ingredients and divide evenly among the hamburger buns. Serves 4.

Not Just a Burger - Hawaiian

Yes, it's unusual. But you'll get raves!

2 lbs ground chuck
1 can chunk pineapple, drained

Make eight thin hamburger patties. Divide pineapple chunks onto four of the patties. Cover with the remaining four hamburger patties, sealing well.

Place on a double thickness of heavy duty aluminum foil. Salt and pepper to taste. Seal pockets tightly and place on a grate over hot coals.

Cook for 15 to 20 minutes, then turn pockets over. Continue cooking for an additional 15 to 20 minutes. Serves 4.

Not Just a Burger - Irish

In honor of my Uncle Howard, I used Idaho potatoes.

2 lbs ground chuck
1 large potato, pared and diced
4 green onions, sliced

Make eight thin hamburger patties. Divide diced potatoes and onions onto four of the patties. Cover with the remaining four hamburger patties, sealing well.

Place on a double thickness of heavy duty aluminum foil. Salt and pepper to taste. Seal pockets tightly and place on a grate over hot coals.

Cook for 15 to 20 minutes, then turn pockets over. Continue cooking for an additional 15 to 20 minutes. Serves 4.

Not Just a Burger - Italian

Even the Godfather would approve.

2 lbs ground chuck
1 onion, diced
8 Tbsp spaghetti sauce
1 cup mozzarella cheese, shredded
Salt and pepper, to taste

Make eight thin hamburger patties. Divide onions, spaghetti sauce, and cheese on four of the patties. Cover with the remaining four hamburger patties, sealing well.

Place on a double thickness of heavy duty aluminum foil. Salt and pepper to taste. Seal pockets tightly and place on a grate over hot coals. Cook for 15 to 20 minutes, then turn pockets over. Continue cooking for an additional 15 to 20 minutes. Serves 4.

Not Just a Burger - South Texas

2 lbs ground chuck
1 onion, diced
1 can red beans, drained
Chili powder to taste
Jalapeno peppers, if desired
Salt and pepper, to taste
4 slices Montery Jack cheese

Make eight thin hamburger patties. Divide next four ingredients on half of the patties. Cover with the remaining four patties, sealing well. Place on a double thickness of heavy duty aluminum foil; season to taste. Seal tightly. Cook on a grate over hot coals for 15-20 minutes. Turn pockets over and cook for an additional 15-20 minutes. Open pockets, top burgers with cheese, and heat until the cheese begins to melt. Serves 4.

Outdoor Nachos

Good anytime . . . sure to please.

1 pkg (14.5 oz) white corn tortilla chips
$1^1/_2$ lbs. ground chuck
2 cans (11 oz) cheddar cheese soup
1 small jar (8 oz) thick and chunky salsa
$^1/_2$ cup red peppers, chopped
$^1/_2$ cup green onions, sliced
Salt and pepper, to taste
Jalapeno peppers, if desired

Brown hamburger in a foil skillet on a grate over hot coals. Stir to crumble. When browned, drain off grease.

Add soup and picante sauce. Heat through. Pour over tortilla chips, then sprinkle on red peppers and green onions. Serves 6.

Ready When You Are Sandwich

On the run? This deli-style meal is ready in just minutes.

$^1/_2$ loaf Italian bread, sliced lengthwise
4 oz pepper beef slices
4 oz corned beef slices
4 oz pepperoni slices
2 tomatoes, sliced
1 red onion, sliced
3 Tbsp creamy Italian salad dressing
4 oz colby cheese

Stack ingredients on bread in the order given so the bread will not become soggy.

Wrap in aluminum foil and place in the cooler. As people come back to camp, the loaf can be pulled out, the desired amount sliced off, and the rest returned to the cooler. Serves 4-6.

Reuben Melt

You don't have to be home to fix this stand-by.

8 slices rye bread
16 slices corned beef
1 cup sauerkraut
Thousand Island dressing, to taste
4 slices cheese
3 Tbsp margarine

Heat a foil skillet on a grate over medium-hot coals. Butter one side of each slice of bread. Place four slices of bread, butter side down, in the heated foil skillet. Stack with corned beef, sauerkraut, dressing, and cheese, and cover with remaining four slices of bread. Grill until both sides are golden brown and cheese is melted. Serves 4.

South of the Border BLT's

Bet you have to make more!

12 flour tortillas (burrito size)
1 lb bacon
3 cups lettuce, shredded
3 tomatoes, chopped
Mayonnaise, to taste

Fry bacon in a foil skillet on a grate over hot coals until golden brown and crisp. Drain on paper towels.

Place two slices of bacon down the center of each tortilla, top with lettuce, tomatoes, and mayonnaise. Roll and enjoy. Serves 4 - 6.

Steak Sandwich

Time and again, a camp favorite.

8 slices favorite bread
4 breakfast steaks
8 slices bacon
4 slices favorite cheese
2 medium onions, cut into rings
3 Tbsp vegetable oil

Fry bacon in a foil skillet on a grate over medium hot coals. Drain on paper towels and set aside.

Heat oil in a foil pan on a grate over hot coals. Add steak and onions. Cook until the steak is nicely browned on both sides and onions are tender. Serve on bread or toast. Serves 4.

Stews, Chilies

30 Minute
Chicken Stew

2 5-oz cans chunk white chicken
1 onion, diced
1 8-oz can tomato sauce
1 8-oz can water
1 15-oz can corn, drained
1 15-oz can lima beans, drained
2 15-oz cans whole potatoes, drained
2 Tbsp pimentos, chopped
Salt and pepper, to taste

Place all ingredients in a foil pot on a grate over hot coals. Cook until onions are tender. Serves 4.

Beefy Chili

Try it with pork, too.

$1^1/_2$ lbs stew meat, cut into small pieces
1 onion, diced
1 15-oz can chili-style chunky tomatoes
1 15-oz can red beans
2 Tbsp chili powder, or   to taste
Salt and pepper, to taste

Brown stew meat in a small amount of vegetable oil in a foil pot on a grate over hot coals. Add remaining ingredients and simmer until meat is tender. Serves 4 - 6.

Hunter's Stew
with Dumplings

2 lbs stew meat
2 lg onions, diced
4 lg carrots, sliced
2 stalks celery, sliced
4 lg potatoes, pared/diced
1 46-oz can tomato juice

Fashion a large foil pot from four thicknesses of heavy duty aluminum foil.
Place stew meat and $1^1/_2$ quarts water in the pot and bring to a simmer.
Salt and pepper to taste. Simmer for one hour, adding water as needed.

Add remaining ingredients; bring to a simmer. Adjust seasonings, if
necessary. Simmer an additional hour, or until meat and vegetables are
tender.

Dumplings: Prepare biscuit mix by following package directions. Drop
by spoonfuls onto the stew. Simmer covered for 10 minutes, then uncovered 10 minutes. Serves 6.

Italian Pork Stew

2 Tbsp vegetable oil
$1^1/_2$ lbs boneless pork loin, cut into 1" cubes
1 onion, chopped
1 sweet yellow pepper, seeded and cut into strips
1 sweet red pepper, seeded and cut into strips
1 can (14.5 oz) diced tomatoes
1 Tbsp dried basil
1 Tbsp fresh parsley, chopped
Salt and pepper, to taste
2-3 cups hot cooked rice

Set a foil pot on a grate over hot coals. Brown pork in vegetable oil. Add onion and peppers; cook until tender. Pour in tomatoes and season with basil, parsley, salt and pepper. Cover and simmer for 20-30 minutes, or until pork is done and tender, stirring occasionally. Serve over rice. Serves 4-6.

Italian Sausage Stew
A little taste of Italy

4 Italian sausages, cut into $^1/_2$" slices
1 onion, cut into 6 wedges
1 can (11 oz.) Italiam tomato soup
$^1/_2$ cup water
1 cup carrots, sliced
$^1/_2$ cup celery, sliced
8 new potatoes, halved
Salt and pepper, to taste

Place a foil skillet on a grate over medium-hot coals. Brown sausages in skillet. Add remaining ingredients and cook for 25-30 minutes, or until vegetables are tender. Serves 4.

Lori's Chili

Not too hot . . . not too tame.

$1^1/_2$ lbs ground chuck
1 lg white onion, diced
2 cans (15.5 oz) red beans
1 can (15 oz) tomato sauce
1 can (15 oz) water
2 Tbsp chili powder, or to taste
Salt and pepper, to taste

Brown hamburger and onion in a foil skillet on a grate over hot coals. Stir to crumble; drain off grease.

Combine all ingredients in a foil pot over hot coals; simmer for 20 to 25 minutes.

Before serving, top with corn chips and shredded cheddar cheese. Serves 4 - 6.

New Orleans Cheese Soup

This is a thick and hearty soup perfect for days with a chill in the air.

1 cup milk
1 16-oz pkg processed cheese, cut into cubes
1 11-oz can mexi-corn, drained
1 15.5-oz can black beans, drained
1 14.25-oz can diced tomatoes
1 Tbsp tabasco sauce (or to taste)

Pour 1 inch of water in a foil pan on grate over hot coals; heat until water is hot.

Place all ingredients in a foil pot and set in the pan of water on the grate. Cook over hot coals, stirring frequently until cheese is melted and soup is hot. Serves 4-6.

No Meat Chili
Even non-vegetarians will like it!

2 cans (15 oz.) chunky chili tomato sauce
1 sweet red pepper, seeded and diced
1 onion, diced
2 cups broccoli florets
1 can (14.5 oz) kernel corn, drained
1 can (15.5 oz) spicy chili beans
1 can (4.5 oz) green chilies, chopped
Salt and pepper, to taste

Place a foil pot on a grate over medium-hot coals. Add all ingredients to the pot. Simmer until broccoli and onions are tender.

Before serving, top each serving with grated, low-fat cheddar cheese. Serves 6.

Tex-Mex Chili
with Cornbread Dumplings

2 lbs ground chuck
1 lg onion, diced
1 11-oz can mexi-corn
1 15-oz can chili tomatoes
1 red pepper, diced
1 yellow pepper, diced
1 15-oz can red beans

Brown hamburger in a foil skillet on a grate over hot coals. Stir to crumble; drain off grease. Combine all ingredients in a foil pot on a grate over hot coals; simmer for 20 to 25 minutes.

Dumplings: Prepare cornbread muffin mix according to package directions. Drop by spoonfuls onto chili. Cook, covered, 10 minutes and uncovered, 10 minutes. Serves 6 - 8.

Wayne's Chili

For the Wayne in many of you.
This one has some bite to it.

$1^1/_2$ lbs ground chuck
1 lg onion, diced
1 15-oz can kidney beans
1 15-oz can pork and beans
1 15-oz can tomatoes, chopped
1 cup thick and chunky salsa
Salt and pepper, to taste

Brown hamburger and onion in a foil skillet on a grate over hot coals.
Stir to crumble; drain off grease. Combine hamburger, onion, and all
remaining ingredients in a foil pot on a grate over hot coals and simmer
for 20 to 25 minutes. Serves 4 - 6.

Beef

American/Spanish Rice
Mild, ethnic blend

2 lbs ground chuck
1 lg onion, diced
1 16-oz can tomatoes, chopped
1 cup Minute® rice, uncooked
$^3/_4$ cup ketchup
2 cups water
Salt and pepper, to taste

Brown hamburger and onion in a foil skillet on a grate over hot coals; drain grease. Place hamburger and onion mixture in the bottom of a foil pot and add rice, tomatoes, ketchup, salt, pepper, and water. Cook, without stirring, on a grate over medium hot coals, until rice is tender. Add more water if necessary. Serves 6-8.

Barbecued Meatloaf on the Grill
Good smoky flavor

2 lbs ground chuck
1 onion, finely chopped
$^1/_4$ cup parsley, chopped
2 carrots, grated
$^3/_4$ tsp salt
$^1/_4$ tsp pepper
$^1/_2$ cup bread crumbs
2 eggs
$^1/_2$ cup ketchup
Favorite barbecue sauce

Combine all ingredients, except barbecue sauce. Shape into 6 patties. Place on a double thickness of heavy duty aluminum foil and seal. Place pocket on a grate over hot coals. Cook for 45 to 60 minutes, or until meat is done. Carefully remove meat from pocket and place on thecooking grate. Brush liberally with your favorite barbecue sauce. Cook 5 minutes, turn once. Baste other side with barbecue sauce and cook for 5 more minutes. Serves 6.

Beef Burgundy

1 lb top sirloin, thinly sliced
2 cloves garlic, minced
$^1/_2$ tsp dried thyme
2 Tbsp olive oil
1 can sliced mushrooms, drained
1 can (14.5 oz) diced tomatoes, drained
1 can (8 oz) tomato sauce
3/4 cup dry red wine
Salt and pepper, to taste
Cooked egg noodles

Heat olive oil in a foil pot on a grate placed over medium-hot coals. Add sirloin and garlic; saute until browned on all sides.

Add remaining ingredients and cook for 20-25 minutes, stirring 2-3 times. Thicken with 1 Tbsp cornstarch, if desired. Serve over egg noodles and enjoy a glass of wine while dining under the stars. Serves 2-4.

Beef Stroganoff

Oxymoron — "Gourmet camp food"

1 lb sirloin, cut into strips
2 Tbsp vegetable oil
1 onion, diced
1 can (10.5 oz) beef broth
1 small can sliced mushrooms, drained
1 cup sour cream
Cornstarch to thicken

Heat vegetable oil in a foil skillet on a grate over medium hot coals. Add sirloin and onion; cook until browned and tender. Stir in beef broth and mushrooms. Simmer for 15 to 20 minutes, then add just enough cornstarch to thicken the broth. Fold in sour cream and heat an additional 5 to 10 minutes. Serve over egg noodles or rice. Serves 4-6.

Campfire Brisket

1 2-lb beef brisket
$^1/_2$ tsp salt
$^1/_4$ tsp pepper
2 onions, sliced
3 cloves garlic, minced
1 15-oz can diced tomatoes
1 cup ketchup
$^1/_3$ cup brown sugar, packed
1 tsp liquid smoke

Place brisket on grate over hot coals, browning both sides. Remove brisket; sprinkle on salt and pepper. Meanwhile, combine remaining ingredients in a foil bowl; mix well. Place brisket on a double thickness of heavy duty aluminum foil. Pour liquid ingredients over brisket and seal pocket. Place on a grate over medium-hot coals and allow to slow cook $1^1/_2$ to 2 hours or until brisket is fork tender. Remove and let stand 10-15 minutes before cutting into thin slices. Spoon mixture over brisket. Serves 6.

Campfire Hamburger Steak
A favorite with scouts everywhere.

2 lbs ground chuck
2 medium onions, diced
4 medium potatoes, diced
4 large carrots, sliced
Salt and pepper, to taste

Place hamburger on a double thickness of heavy duty aluminum foil. Scatter remaining ingredients in and around the hamburger. Seal the foil pocket.

Place on a grate over hot coals and cook for 45 to 60 minutes, or until the hamburger is done and the vegetables are tender. Drain juices before serving. Serves 4-6.

Chili Rubbed Steak

1 lb boneless top sirloin steak, 1" thick
2 Tbsp chili powder
1 Tbsp paprika
$\frac{1}{2}$ tsp salt
$\frac{1}{4}$ tsp pepper
1 Tbsp vegetable oil
$\frac{1}{2}$ cup sour cream with chives

Combine chili powder, paprika, salt, and pepper in a small foil bowl; mix until well blended. Brush both sides of beef with vegetable oil. Sprinkle seasoning mixture over both sides of steak; using fingers, rub into steak.

Place steak on a grate over medium-hot coals; cover with an aluminum foil tent and cook 15-18 minutes or until steak is of desired doneness, turning once. Remove from fire and let stand 5 minutes, keeping warm. To serve, cut steak diagonally into thin slices; top each serving with sour cream. Serves 4.

Corned Beef Wellington

Tell your friends that you cooked Corned Beef Wellington
beside an open campfire and they will be amazed!
And they said it couldn't be done!

2 12-oz cans corned beef
1 8-oz pkg refrigerator crescent rolls

Roll out dough and divide in half. Roll each half to a 5 x 8-inch rectangle. Wrap each block of corned beef with dough, pinching to seal. Bake in a reflector oven before a very hot fire. Rotate periodically, until crust is done and nicely browned. Serves 4-6.

Drunken Beef

4 slices bacon, cut into 1" strips
1 lb beef stir fry strips
4 medium onions, sliced
$\frac{1}{2}$ cup brown sugar, packed
1 can (12 oz) beer
1 can (14.5 oz.) beef broth
$\frac{1}{4}$ tsp salt
$\frac{1}{8}$ tsp pepper
2 Tbsp cornstarch

Cook bacon until crisp; drain. Cook onions in 1 Tbsp drippings until browned and tender, stirring frequently. Add brown sugar and $^1/_4$ cup beer; simmer for 10 minutes. Remove onions and set aside. Brown beef strips in foil skillet, stirring until thoroughly cooked. Drain. Place all ingredients in a foil pot over medium-hot coals. Simmer until heated through and liquid is slightly thickened. Serve over egg noodles. Serves 4-6.

Garlic Rubbed Roast
Loaded with flavor - gravy is wonderfully tasty

1 2-lb boneless chuck or arm roast
12 new potatoes
2 medium onions, quartered
1 whole garlic, skinned
$^1/_2$ tsp salt
$^1/_2$ tsp pepper
$^1/_2$ tsp paprika
Juice of 1 lime
3 Tbsp Worchestershire sauce
2 Tbsp vegetable oil
2 Tbsp cornstarch

Mash garlic (to form a paste) in a small foil bowl; add salt, pepper and paprika. Mix well.

Meanwhile, brown roast on a grate over medium-hot coals, turning once. Remove and cool slightly. Rub oil and garlic mixture into roast, covering both the sides and the edges.

Arrange the roast on a double thickness of heavy duty aluminum foil. Add lime juice and Worchestershire sauce around the roast; place onions on top. Seal pocket. Place foil pocket on a grate over medium-hot coals. Cook for 1 hour.

Carefully open top of foil pocket (beware of escaping steam as it can cause a severe burn) and add potatoes. Reseal pocket and allow to cook additional 35-40 minutes, or until potatoes are fork tender.

Remove meat, potatoes, and onion from pan drippings and place on a serving platter; keep warm. Stir cornstarch into drippings and cook over coals, stirring constantly, until thickened. Spoon gravy over the roast and serve. Serves 4-6.

German Meatballs

Whatever your homeland, I think you'll enjoy this blend of flavors.

$1^1/_2$ lbs ground chuck
1 cup grated raw potatoes
$^1/_2$ tsp salt
$^1/_4$ tsp pepper
1 onion, finely chopped
1 tsp lemon rind, grated
1 egg
1 $10^1/_2$-oz can beef broth
Cornstarch to thicken

Combine first seven ingredients, mixing well. Form walnut-sized meatballs and place into a foil skillet.

Fry, turning often, to brown all sides, then drain off grease. Add beef broth and cornstarch to meatballs and stir until thickened. Serve over egg noodles. Serves 4.

Good Anytime Stir-Fry

Serve with rice and you're ready
for hungry campers.

$1^1/_2$ lbs ground chuck
2 cups broccoli florets
$^1/_3$ cup green onions, sliced
$^1/_3$ cup carrots, sliced
1 10-oz jar sweet and sour sauce
Salt and pepper, to taste

Brown hamburger in a foil skillet on a grate over hot coals, stirring to crumble. Drain off grease. Add remaining ingredients and simmer until heated through. Serves 6.

Hamburger Steak Fiesta

Olé — very festive.

2 lbs ground chuck
1 small can sliced mushrooms, drained
4 slices colby cheese
2 tomatoes, chopped
8 green onions, sliced
Salt and pepper, to taste

Make four large hamburger patties. Place on a grate over hot coals and grill until well done.

Place hamburgers on a double thickness of heavy duty aluminum foil. Layer with mushrooms and cheese. Cook until the cheese begins to melt.

Serve with tomatoes and green onions sprinkled on top. Serves 4.

Mesquite Smoked Chuck Roast

2 lbs boneless chuck roast
Marinade:
    1 cup cranberry juice
    $^1/_2$ cup orange juice
    2 onions, thinly sliced
    2 cloves garlic, minced
    1 tsp salt
    $^1/_2$ tsp pepper
    1 tsp celery seeds
    4 carrots, sliced

Soak one cup mesquite chips in water for one hour before using. Remove and sprinkle the wet mesquite chips over the hot coals. Brown the chuck roast on a grate over the hot coals. Combine marinade ingredients in a foil pot; stir to blend.

Remove chuck roast from the cooking grate and place in the pot with the marinade. Cover and simmer for 60 to 75 minutes, or until tender. Let stand for 10 minutes, slice, and serve. Serves 6-8.

Mom's Favorite Meatloaf

Mom would be proud.

2 lbs ground chuck
1 large onion, diced
2 eggs
$^3/_4$ cup quick oats, uncooked
1 cup ketchup
$^1/_2$ tsp salt
$^1/_4$ tsp pepper

Combine all ingredients, reserving $^1/_2$ cup ketchup. Form mixture into round or oblong loaf. Place on a double thickness of aluminum foil and seal.

Place on a grate over hot coals and cook for 60 minutes or until done in the center. Open pocket and spread remaining ketchup on top of meatloaf. Cook, with foil open, for additional 15 minutes. Serves 6.

Onion Surprise Bake

2 lbs ground chuck
1 cup Minute© rice
2 eggs
1 tsp salt
$^1/_4$ tsp pepper
6 medium onions

Cut onions in half, vertically. Remove centers, leaving quarter-inch shells. Dice onion centers.

Combine hamburger, rice, eggs, diced onions, salt, and pepper. Spoon mixture into onion halves.

Place two onion halves together and set on a double thickness of aluminum foil. Seal, and place on a grate over hot coals. Cook for 20 minutes, turn pockets over, and continue cooking for another 20 minutes, or until onions are tender and hamburger is done. Serves 6.

Peppercorn Roast
Full bodied aroma and flavor

1 beef rump roast (2$^1/_2$ lb)
1 tsp salt
$^1/_4$ cup peppercorns, crushed
1 large onion, sliced
1 can (10.75 oz) cream of onion soup
$^1/_4$ cup water

Rub salt into roast. Place on a double thickness of heavy duty aluminum foil. Press peppercorns into roast, top with onion slices.

Combine water and onion soup. Pour at base of roast. Seal pocket. Place on a grate over medium-hot coals for 1-1/2 to 2 hours. When done, allow roast to stand 10-15 minutes before slicing. Serve with onion gravy drizzled on top. Serves 6.

Rotini Goulash
Subtle blend of flavors

1 lb extra lean ground beef
1 cup chopped onion
1 cup chopped celery
1 can (14.5 oz) diced tomatoes, undrained
1 can (10.75-oz) condensed tomato soup
3 cups rotini noodles, cooked
$^1/_2$ cup sour cream
$^1/_2$ tsp salt
$^1/_4$ tsp pepper

Brown hamburger, onions, celery, salt and pepper in foil skillet on a grate over hot coals. Drain off grease. Add tomatoes and tomato soup, stirring to mix.

Transfer hamburger mixture to foil pot. Add cooked rotini noodles; simmer for 10 minutes. Stir in sour cream until blended and goulash is hot. Serve immediately. Serves 6.

Shepherd's Pie

Heat a jar of brown gravy to spoon on top. Then stand by for the compliments.

1 lb ground chuck
1 onion, diced
$1/_2$ cup shredded carrots
$1/_4$ cup celery, diced
3 potatoes, peeled and diced
$1/_3$ cup milk
1 Tbsp margarine
$1/_2$ cup shredded cheese
2 Tbsp vegetable oil

Place a foil skillet on a grate over hot coals; heat oil. Sauté onions and celery till tender, then add hamburger; stir to crumble. When browned, drain off grease and add carrots. Divide into four individual, serving-sized foil pots.

Meanwhile, boil potatoes until tender. Drain, add margarine, and milk. Season to taste with salt and pepper.Mash potatoes until smooth, add cheese and stir. Spread mashed potatoes over hamburger mixture and place in foil reflector oven. Bake until potatoes are golden brown. Serves 4.

Spanish Rice

2 lbs ground chuck
1 lg onion, diced
1 cup Minute® rice, uncooked
$^1/_2$ cup chunky picante sauce
2 cups water
Salt and pepper to taste

Brown hamburger and onions in a foil skillet on a grate over hot coals; drain grease. Place hamburger and onion mixture in the bottom of a foil pot and add rice, picante sauce, salt, pepper, and water. Cook, without stirring, on a grate over medium hot coals, until rice is tender. Add more water, if necessary. Serves 6-8.

Steak Italian

We surprised some "hot-dog-on-a-stick" campers with this recipe.

4 cube steaks
4 small potatoes, diced
2 onions, diced
1 cup spaghetti sauce
4 slices mozzarella cheese
Salt and pepper, to taste

Place the first four ingredients on 4 sheets (double thickness) of heavy duty aluminum foil in the order given. Salt and pepper to taste.

Seal foil pockets and place on a grate over hot coals. Cook for 45 minutes. Carefully, open pockets and place cheese on top of the steak. Continue cooking for an additional 5 to 10 minutes, or until cheese is melted. Serves 4.

Stuffed Cabbage Rolls

You don't have to go to Grandma's house for this anymore.

1 head cabbage
2 lbs ground chuck
1 cup Minute® rice
1 onion, diced
$^3/_4$ tsp salt
$^1/_4$ tsp pepper
1 can (8 oz) tomato sauce
3 Tbsp margarine
Cornstarch to thicken

Wilt 12 large cabbage leaves in a foil pot of boiling water on a grate over hot coals. Drain and set aside.

Combine hamburger, rice, onion, salt, and pepper. Divide mixture into 12 oblong patties. Wrap each patty with the cabbage leaves. Place side by side on a double thickness of heavy duty aluminum foil. Cover with tomato 12 oblong patties. Wrap each patty with the cabbage leaves. Place side by side on a double thickness of heavy duty aluminum foil. Cover with tomato 12 oblong patties. Wrap each patty with the cabbage leaves. Place side by side on a double thickness of heavy duty aluminum foil. Cover with tomatotomato sauce, margarine, and $^1/_3$ cup water. Seal foil and place on a grate over hot coals. Cook for 45 minutes. Drain juice into a small foil pan and stir in just enough cornstarch to thicken. Serve sauce over cabbage rolls. Serves 6.

Swiss Steak

1 round steak, $^1/_2$-inch thick
2 onions, sliced
2 stalks celery, sliced
15-oz can tomatoes, chopped
2 tsp Worcestershire sauce
Salt and pepper, to taste

Place steak on a double thickness of heavy duty aluminum foil. Add remaining ingredients; seal foil pocket. Place on a grate over hot coals and cook until meat is tender.

Note: The longer the round steak is cooked, sealed in foil, the more tender it will become. Serves 6.

Pork

Cajun Pork

The meat and vegetables have a wonderful sweet/sour taste.

2 lbs boneless pork roast
1 12-oz jar pineapple preserves
2 Tbsp cajun spices
2 onions, quartered
2 potatoes, quartered
4-6 carrots, sliced
$^1/_2$ cup brown sugar
Salt and pepper, to taste

Place pork roast on a double thickness of heavy duty aluminum foil. Rub cajun spices, salt, and pepper into the meat. Place remaining ingredients on and around the roast.

Seal the foil pocket and place on a grate over medium-hot coals. Cook slowly for $1^1/_2$ to 2 hours, or until tender. The juices can be thickened with corn starch and used as a gravy, if desired. Serves 6.

Campfire Tamale Pie

Can't beat this one for good taste.

1 lb ground chuck
1 15-oz can tamales
1 onion, diced
1 clove garlic, minced
1 16-oz can chili beans
1 cup corn chips, crushed
$^3/_4$ cup cheddar cheese, shredded
Salt and pepper to taste

Brown hamburger, onion, and garlic in a foil skillet on a grate over hot coals, stirring to crumble. Drain off grease. Place hamburger mixture in a foil pot. Layer beans, tamales, cheese and corn chips on top. Cover, and heat until cheese melts. Serves 6.

Country Pork Ribs with Cranberry Sauce

"A close runner-up," says Ranger Ron.

4-5 lbs meaty country pork ribs
1 16-oz can cranberry sauce
$^2/_3$ cup brown sugar
Salt and pepper to taste

Rub salt and pepper into the ribs. Place on a double thickness of heavy duty aluminum foil. Add cranberry sauce and brown sugar. Seal pocket.

Place foil pocket on a grate over hot coals. Cook for 60 minutes, or until tender. The sauce is good drizzled over rice. Serves 6.

Gingered Pork

Wild rice makes a nice accompaniment

2 pork tenderloins, $^3/_4$ lb each.
$^1/_2$ cup apple jelly
1 Tbsp ginger root, grated
2 Tbsp Worchestershire sauce
1 clove garlic, minced
Salt and pepper, to taste

Place pork on a double thickness of heavy duty aluminum foil. Combine remaining ingredients, spoon over meat, and seal pocket.

Place pocket on a grate over medium-hot coals. Cook for 50-60 Minutes, or until pork is done and tender. Serves 6.

Ham Steak with Sweet Potatoes

Bet you have this more than once.

1 center cut ham steak
2 large sweet potatoes, pared and quartered
2 tart apples, cored and sliced
$^1/_2$ cup raisins
$^3/_4$ cup brown sugar
2 Tbsp margarine

Place all ingredients on a double thickness of heavy duty aluminum foil in the order given. Seal pocket.

Place foil pocket on a grate over hot coals. Cook 45 to 50 minutes, or until sweet potatoes and apples are tender. Serves 4.

Ham Sweetened with Pineapple

1 ham steak, $^3/_4$" thick
1 15.25-oz can pineapple tidbits, undrained
$^1/_4$ cup brown sugar, packed
$^1/_4$ cup raisins
$^1/_4$ tsp ground cloves
$^1/_4$ tsp nutmeg
$^1/_4$ tsp cinnamon

Brown ham steak on a grate over medium-hot coals, turning once; set aside. Combine remaining ingredients; mix well.

Place ham steak on a double thickness of heavy duty aluminum foil. Cover with pineapple mixture and seal pocket. Place pocket on the fire grate and cook for 35-40 minutes over medium-hot coals, or until pineapple mixture is caramelized and slightly thickened. To serve, divide ham into 4 servings. Stir pineapple mixture and spoon over ham. Serves 4.

Italian Sausage

Choose your favorite — mild
or hot Italian sausage. Either
way, the flavor is superb.

6 Italian sausages
1 15-oz can tomato sauce
1 1.5-oz pkg spaghetti seasoning

Brown sausage in a foil skillet on a grate over medium-hot coals, turning several times. Add tomato sauce and spaghetti seasoning. Cover and continue cooking, stirring occasionally, for 30 minutes to allow flavors to mix. Serve over your favorite pasta. Serves 6.

Most Tender Country Ribs

Ranger Ron's favorite.

4-5 lbs meaty country pork ribs

2 cups ketchup

1 Tbsp liquid smoke

$^3/_4$ cup brown sugar

1 tart apple, thinly sliced

Place ribs on a double thickness of heavy duty aluminum foil. Add remaining ingredients and seal pocket.

Place on a grate over hot coals. Cook for 60 minutes, or until ribs are fully cooked and tender.

If you prefer a caramelized crust, remove ribs from the foil pocket and continue cooking directly on the grate for an additional 10 to 15 minutes. Serves 6.

Peachy Ham Glaze

Ham has never tasted better

1 center cut ham steak

$^3/_4$ cup peach preserves

$^1/_2$ cup brown sugar

$^1/_2$ tsp ground ginger

Place all ingredients on a double thickness of heavy duty aluminum foil in the order given. Seal pocket.

Place foil pocket on a grate over hot coals. Cook for 30 to 45 minutes, or until the ham is tender. Serves 4.

Plum Good Pork Chops

Next time, use plum preserves. The taste is the same
but it's more eye-appealing when served.

4-8 pork chops, cut $^3/_4$-inch thick
$^1/_2$ 6-oz jar plum jelly
$^1/_3$ cup brown sugar
Salt and pepper, to taste

Place chops on a double thickness of heavy duty aluminum foil. Combine jelly and brown sugar. Spread on top of chops. Season with salt and pepper.

Seal foil pockets and place on grate over hot coals. Cook for 45 to 50 minutes, or until pork is done and tender. Serves 4-8.

Pork 'N Apricots

This roast is so juicy, it will
simply melt in your mouth.

2 lbs boneless pork roast
1 12-oz jar apricot preserves
$^1/_2$ cup brown sugar
2 large sweet potatoes, cut into strips
2 Tbsp dried flaked parsley
Salt and pepper, to taste

Rub pork roast with salt, pepper, and parsley flakes. Place on a double thickness of heavy duty aluminum foil. Arrange remaining ingredients on and around the roast, then seal pocket.

Place foil pocket on a grate over medium hot coals and cook slowly for $1^1/_2$ to 2 hours, or until the pork is tender. Serves 6.

Pork and Onions Galore

Carma, this one's for you.

2 lbs pork tenderloin, cut into strips
1 red onion, sliced
1 white onion, sliced
1 yellow onion, sliced
6 green onions, sliced
$^1/_2$ cup teriyaki sauce
1 tomato, chopped, and seeds removed
3 Tbsp vegetable oil
Salt and pepper, to taste

Heat oil in a foil skillet on a grate over hot coals. Add pork strips. Brown on all sides. Add remaining ingredients; simmer for 20 minutes. Serve over hot rice. Serves 4-6.

Pork and Oranges

Hands down, it's a winner!

$1^1/_2$ lb pork loin, cut into four pieces
$^1/_2$ cup orange marmalade
$^1/_3$ cup brown sugar

Place pork on a double thickness of heavy duty aluminum foil. Cover with marmalade and brown sugar. Seal pocket.

Place foil pocket on a grate over hot coals. Cook for 45 minutes, or until pork is tender. Serves 4.

Pork Steak
with Apples and Raisins

A sure-fire, blue ribbon winner.

4 pork steaks
2 tart cooking apples, cored and sliced
$1/_3$ cup raisins
1 Tbsp margarine
$1/_2$ cup brown sugar
Salt and pepper, to taste

Brown pork steaks on a grate over hot coals, turning once.

Arrange meat on a double thickness of heavy duty aluminum foil. Cover with remaining ingredients and seal pocket.

Place foil pocket on a grate over hot coals. Cook for 35 to 40 minutes, or until pork is done and tender. Serves 4.

Quick Beans
'N Ham

Perfect on a chilly day

3 11.5-oz cans bean with bacon soup
3 cans water
$1/_2$ lb ham chunks
$1/_4$ cup shredded carrots

Place all ingredients in a foil pot on a grate over medium-hot coals. Bring to a simmer and cook for 15 minutes. Serve with or over cornbread. Serves 6.

Sausage and Cherries

Flavor is everything

6 Italian sausages, hot or mild
1 jar cherry preserves

Place sausages and preserves on a double thickness of heavy duty aluminum foil. Seal pocket.

Place foil pocket on a grate over hot coals. Cook for 45 to 50 minutes or until sausage is done. Sauce is delicious drizzled over rice. Serves 6.

Stick To Your Ribs - Ribs

Simmered in a tangy sauce

3 lbs pork country style ribs
1 cup ketchup
$1/_3$ cup orange marmalade
1 Tbsp onion, minced
1 Tbsp Worchestershire sauce
$1/_2$ tsp celery seed
1 Tbsp hot pepper sauce
$1/_4$ cup brown sugar, packed
Hot cooked rice

Brown ribs on a grate over hot coals, turning once. Arrange browned ribs on a double thickness of heavy duty aluminum foil.

Combine remaining ingredients in a foil bowl, mixing thoroughly. Pour sauce over ribs and seal pocket. Place on a grate over medium-hot coals and cook for $1^1/_2$ hours, or until fork-tender. Serve ribs on bed of rice with sauce drizzled over top. Serves 4-6.

Stuffed Pork Cutlet Roll-ups

6 tenderized pork cutlets
1 box stuffing mix, prepared
$^1/_2$ red pepper, diced
$^1/_2$ yellow pepper, diced
1 onion, diced
1 can cream of mushroom soup

Prepare stuffing mix according to package directions in a foil pot on a grate over hot coals. Remove from fire.

Add peppers and onion to the stuffing. Spread mixture down the center of the pork cutlets. Roll up, securing with toothpick, if necessary.

Place cutlets on a double thickness of heavy duty aluminum foil and cover with mushroom soup. Seal foil pockets and set on a grate over hot coals. Cook for 45 minutes or until pork is done. Serves 6.

Sweet and Sour Chops
Special meat and fruit blend

4 boneless loin pork chops,   1" thick
1 tart apple, diced
$^1/_2$ cup applesauce
1 small can saurkraut, drained and rinsed
$^1/_4$ cup orange juice
$^1/_4$ cup brown sugar, packed
Salt and pepper, to taste

Brown pork chops on a grate over hot coals, turning once. Lightly salt and pepper both sides.

Place browned chops on a double thickness of heavy duty aluminum foil. Combine remaining ingredients; spoon over chops. Seal pocket. Place the foil pocket on the fire grate and cook over medium-hot coals for 35-40 minutes, or until chops are done and tender. Serves 4.

Sweet and Sour Pork Stir-Fry

1 lb lean pork medallions, cut into thin strips
1 egg
$1/4$ cup milk
Flour
Vegetable oil
$1/4$ cup carrots, shredded
$1/2$ green pepper, cut into strips
1 10-oz jar sweet sour sauce

Beat egg and milk in a foil bowl until smooth. Dip pork strips into batter, shake off excess, and dredge with flour.

Heat vegetable oil in a foil pan on a grate over hot coals. Add pork strips and stir fry until golden brown and cooked completely through. Stir in carrots, pepper, and sweet sour sauce. Continue cooking until thoroughly heated. Serves 4.

Tender Pork Fry

This recipe hits the spot with all who have tried it.

1 lb lean pork loin chops, cut into strips
2 Tbsp soy sauce
3 Tbsp Worchestershire sauce
1 14.5-oz can vegetable broth
2 cans (14.5-oz each) mixed vegetables, undrained
2 cups cooked rice
$1/4$ tsp pepper
1-2 Tbsp cornstarch
Hot cooked rice

Brown pork strips in soy and Worchestershire sauces in foil skillet on grate placed over hot coals. Add vegetable broth; simmer until pork is tender. Add mixed vegetables, pepper and cornstarch. Continue simmering until heated through and slightly thickened. Serve over rice. Serves 4.

Tenderloin with Mushrooms

1 lb pork tenderloin
1 10.75-oz can golden mushroom soup
1 tart apple, cored and sliced
1 stalk celery, sliced
$^1/_4$ tsp caraway seed
$^1/_4$ cup apple jelly

Place pork tenderloin on a grate over hot coals, turning until browned on all sides. Remove from grate and place on a double thickness of heavy duty aluminum foil. Combine remaining ingredients and spread over browned pork.

Seal foil pocket; place on the fire grate and cook for 40-45 minutes over medium-hot coals, or until pork is done and apples are soft. Let stand 10 minutes before slicing. Spoon sauce over meat before serving. Serves 4.

Poultry

Apple Good Chicken
Farm good taste

4 skinless, boneless chicken breasts
4 tart apples, cored and quartered
$^1/_2$ cup plum jelly
$^1/_2$ cup brown sugar
1 Tbsp margarine
Salt and pepper, to taste

Place chicken on a double thickness of aluminum foil. Arrange remaining ingredients on top of, and around, chicken. Seal pocket.

Set the foil pocket on a grate over hot coals and cook for 45 to 50 minutes, or until chicken is done. Serve with rice. Serves 4.

Bacon Flavored Chicken
Take a bow, they'll love it

4 skinless, boneless chicken breasts
4 slices bacon, cooked
4 potatoes, quartered
4 carrots, sliced
Salt and pepper, to taste

Place each chicken breast on its own double thick sheet of heavy duty aluminum foil. Arrange the remaining ingredients on top of, and around, the chicken. Seal pockets.

Set foil packets on a grate over hot coals and cook for 45 to 50 minutes, or until chicken is done. Drain juices. Serve with brown rice. Serves 4.

Chicken Cordon Bleu in the Woods

4 skinless, boneless chicken breast halves

1 can cream of chicken soup

$^1/_3$ can water

4 slices boiled ham

4 slices Swiss cheese

3 Tbsp margarine

Salt and pepper, to taste

Grill chicken breasts on a grate over hot coals. Baste with margarine while grilling. When done, place chicken on a double thickness of heavy duty aluminum foil and cover with chicken soup. Seal pocket.

Place pocket on the cooking grate over hot coals and continue cooking for 5 to 10 minutes. Top with boiled ham and cheese; cook until cheese is melted. Serves 4.

Chicken El Paso
Chicken with a bite

4 skinless, boneless chicken breasts, cubed

4 potatoes, diced

1 11-oz can mexi-corn

1 cup thick and chunky salsa

2 Tbsp vegetable oil

Salt and pepper, to taste

Heat vegetable oil in a foil skillet on a grate over hot coals. Add chicken and potatoes. Cook, stirring occasionally, until chicken is browned and potatoes are tender.

Add salsa, corn, salt, and pepper. Cook for an additional 5 to 10 minutes, or until heated through. Serve over rice. Serves 4.

Chicken Stroganoff

4 skinless, boneless chicken breasts, cut into strips
2 Tbsp vegetable oil
1 onion, diced
1 2-oz jar pimentos, drained and chopped
1 can cream of chicken soup
$^1/_3$ can of water
Salt and pepper, to taste

Heat vegetable oil in a foil pan on a grate over hot coals. Add chicken strips. Cook, turning occasionally, until the meat is lightly browned and cooked all the way through.

Add onion; stir fry for an additional 5 to 10 minutes. Add remaining ingredients. Continue cooking until heated through. Serve over egg noodles or rice. For garnish, sprinkle with minced, fresh parsley. Serves 4.

Chicken with Apple Stuffing
Hats off to the chef!

4 skinless, boneless chicken breasts
1 onion, chopped
1 tart apple, cored and diced
$^1/_2$ cup raisins
$^1/_4$ cup bread crumbs, dry
2 Tbsp margarine
Salt and pepper, to taste

Coating:
  1 egg
  $^1/_4$ cup milk
  $^3/_4$ cup fine dry bread crumbs
  Margarine for basting

Flatten chicken with flat blade of knife to a $^1/_4$-inch thickness. Season with salt and pepper.

Combine onions, apple, raisins, $^1/_4$ cup bread crumbs and 2 Tbsp margarine. Spread down the center of each chicken breast and roll up. Fasten with toothpicks if necessary.

Meanwhile, combine milk and egg in a foil pot. Dip rolled chicken in mixture and coat with crushed bread crumbs. Place on a double thickness of heavy duty aluminum foil. Seal pocket.

Place the foil pocket on a grate over hot coals. Cook, basting occasionally with margarine, until the chicken is cooked completely through, about 45 to 50 minutes. Serves 4.

Chicken with Cheddar Broccoli Rice
A lighter meal with real flair.

4 skinless boneless chicken breasts
2 4.5-oz pkgs cheddar broccoli rice with sauce
2 Tbsp margarine
Salt and pepper, to taste

Place chicken on a double thickness of heavy duty aluminum foil. Dot with margarine; salt and pepper to taste. Seal pockets and place on a grate over hot coals. Check for doneness after 45 minutes.

Meanwhile, place a foil pot on grate over hot coals. Cook cheddar broccoli rice mix according to package directions. Serve with chicken. Serves 4.

Cornish Hens
Bragging rights allowed

4 Cornish hens, thawed
4 small onions, quartered
4 cloves garlic
8 Tbsp margarine
Vegetable oil
Salt and pepper, to taste

Thoroughly clean and rinse the Cornish hens; pat dry. Fill the cavity of each hen with onions, garlic, and margarine. Rub the outside of the hens with vegetable oil, salt, and pepper. Place each hen on its own double thick sheet of heavy duty aluminum foil. Seal pockets.

Set foil pockets on a grate over hot coals. Cook for at least 30 minutes longer than package directions indicate. Serve with brown rice. Serves 4.

Corn Flake Chicken
The kids will love this one!

4 boneless, skinless chicken breast halves, cut into 1" cubes
3 Tbsp vegetable oil
3 green onions, thinly sliced
1 carrot, grated
$1/_2$ tsp paprika
Salt and pepper, to taste
2 cups corn flakes

Heat oil in foil skillet on a grate over medium-hot coals. Add chicken; stir-fry until chicken is no longer pink in the center and outside is nicely browned. Add green onions, grated carrot, paprika, salt and pepper. Stir until onions and carrots are tender. Add corn flakes; stir until heated through. Serves 4.

Grilled Chicken with Orange Glaze

4 skinless, boneless chicken breasts
1 12-oz jar orange marmalade
$^1/_2$ cup brown sugar
1 Tbsp margarine
Salt and pepper, to taste

Place all ingredients on a double thickness of heavy duty aluminum foil. Seal pocket.

Place the foil pocket on a grate over hot coals. Cook 45 to 50 minutes, or until chicken is done.

If you prefer crispy chicken, remove it from the foil pocket. Place directly on the cooking grate over hot coals. Cook for 10 to 15 minutes, turning once. Serve over hot rice. Serves 4.

Golden Dijon Chicken
The sauce says it all

4 boneless, skinless chicken breast halves
1 tsp Italian seasoning, crushed
$^1/_8$ tsp ground red pepper
1 can (10.75 oz) chicken dijon soup

Place chicken on a grate over medium-hot coals; brown both sides. Remove from grate and arrange on a double thickness of heavy duty aluminum foil.

Combine remaining ingredients and spread over chicken; seal pocket. Place foil pocket on a grate over medium-hot coals and cook 25-30 minutes, or until done. Serves 4.

Louisiana Chicken
Mild spicy taste

3 tsp paprika
$^1/_2$ tsp seasoning salt
$^1/_4$ tsp cayenne pepper
4 boneless, skinless chicken breast halves
2 Tbsp olive oil

Combine paprika, seasoning salt, and cayenne; stir to blend. Brush chicken with olive oil, then rub spice mixture evenly over chicken.

Arrange seasoned chicken on a double thickness of heavy duty aluminum foil; seal pocket. Place pocket on a grate over medium-hot coals and cook 10-15 minutes per side, or until chicken is done and juices run clear. Serves 4.

Zesty Orange Chicken

4 boneless, skinless chicken breast halves, cut into strips
2 Tbsp soy sauce
1 garlic clove, minced.
1 small onion, diced
1 sweet yellow pepper strips
1 sweet red pepper strips
$^2/_3$ cup orange juice
1 Tbsp cornstarch
1 orange, peeled, seeded
Salt and pepper, to taste

Stir-fry chicken, soy sauce, garlic, and onion in foil skillet until chicken is nicely browned. Add peppers and cook until tender. Combine orange juice, cornstarch, and orange sections in a foil pot. Cook and stir until mixture is slightly thickened. Stir chicken into orange mixture; simmer until heated through. Season with salt and pepper to taste. Serve over rice. Serves 4.

Fish, Seafood

Alaskan
Salmon Cakes

If you like salmon, you'll love this.

1 14.75-oz can red salmon, deboned
1 pkg saltine crackers (about 40 individual crackers),
    crushed
2 eggs
Salt and pepper, to taste
Margarine

Combine all ingredients in a foil bowl; mix well. Form patties and place on a double thickness of heavy duty aluminum foil. Dot each pattie with margarine. Seal pocket.

Place the foil pocket on a grate over medium-hot coals and cook for 30 to 40 minutes. Serves 4.

Cajun Fish

Louisiana, the northern states love it.

4 perch filets
2 tsp cajun spice, or to taste
2 Tbsp garlic-flavored vegetable oil

Rub fish filets with oil and sprinkle with cajun spice. Place on a large sheet (double thickness) aluminum foil. Seal the foil pocket and place on a grate over hot coals. Allow fish to cook for 10 minutes, turn and cook for an additional 10 minutes, or until fish can be flaked with a fork. Serves 4.

Catfish Fry

As good on the river bank as in the kitchen.

6 catfish fillets
1 cup yellow cornmeal
$^3/_4$ cup flour
2 eggs, beaten
Salt and pepper, to taste
Vegetable oil

Combine cornmeal and flour. Dip fish fillets first in beaten eggs, then dredge in flour mixture. Heat oil in a foil skillet on a grate over hot coals. Add fish and cook until golden brown, turning once. Serves 5.

Crab Cakes

$^1/_2$ cup egg substitute, fat free
1 Tbsp Worchestershire sauce
1 tsp crab seasoning
1 lb imitation crab meat
1 cup plain dry bread crumbs
$^1/_2$ cup sweet red pepper, finely chopped
$^1/_2$ cup green onions, finely sliced
$^1/_4$ cup celery, finely chopped
Salt and pepper, to taste

In a large foil bowl, whisk the egg substitute, Worchestershire sauce, and crab seasoning. Add remaining ingredients and mix well. Shape into 12 patties.

Coat a single sheet of heavy duty aluminum foil with non-fat cooking spray. Place crab cakes on foiled grate over medium-hot coals. Cook until browned, turning once. Serve immediately. Good dipped in low-fat ranch dressing. Serves 6.

Creamed Crab
Cooking in the fast lane!

3 Tbsp margarine
$1/4$ cup all purpose flour
$1/4$ tsp salt
$1/8$ tsp pepper
2 cups milk
1 3-oz pkg cream cheese, cubed
1 can mexi-corn, drained
1 8-oz pkg. chunk style imitation crab
3 Tbsp green onions, sliced
Prepared biscuits

Melt margarine in a foil pot on a grate over medium-hot coals. Stir in flour, salt, and pepper. Add milk and cream cheese. Continue stirring until sauce is smooth and thickened. Add corn and imitation crab, stirring until crab is heated through.

Serve over biscuits; garnish with green onions. Serves 4.

Cucumber Sauce For Fish

1 large cucumber
1 cup sour cream
1 tsp lemon juice
$1/4$ tsp salt
Dash black pepper
$1/2$ tsp dill weed

Peel large cucumber. Cut lengthwise in fourths. Remove seeds and grate. Set aside.

Mix remaining ingredients together; fold in cucumber and stir until mixture is well blended. Chill in cooler until serving time. Makes $1^1/4$ cups sauce.

Henry's Catch

Henry tells me that you can't beat Missouri trout from the Ozarks.

8 (8-10-oz) trout fillets
3 eggs, beaten
2 cups corn flakes, crushed
Salt and pepper, to taste
Vegetable oil

Heat vegetable oil in a foil skillet on a grate over hot coals.

Dip trout fillets in first in the beaten eggs, then roll in corn flakes, coating evenly.

Place fillets in hot oil and cook for 3 to 5 minutes each side, turning only once. Drain on paper toweling and serve hot. Serves 4.

Honey Mustard Catfish Fillets

Fish that smacks good.

4 (8-10-oz) catfish fillets
1 tsp dill weed
4 Tbsp honey mustard
Salt and pepper, to taste

Cover each fillet with honey mustard. Sprinkle with dill, salt, and pepper.

Place fish on a large sheet (double thickness) of aluminum foil. Seal foil pocket and place on a grate over hot coals. Cook fish for 10 minutes, turn, and cook for an additional 10 minutes, or until fish flakes easily when tested with a fork. Serves 4.

Reflector Oven Perch

4 ocean perch fillets (4 oz each)
$^1/_4$ cup dry bread crumbs
2 Tbsp freshly grated parmesan cheese
1 tsp dried basil leaves
$^1/_2$ tsp paprika
2 Tbsp green onions, thinly sliced
2 Tbsp reduced calorie margarine, melted

Spray a sheet of heavy duty aluminum foil with non-stick cooking spray; lay foil in reflector oven. Mix bread crumbs, parmesan cheese, basil leaves, paprika, and green onions. Brush fish with melted margarine; dip into crumb mixture. Place fish on foil in reflector oven and bake 12-15 minutes, or until fish flakes easily with fork. Serves 4.

Salmon on Toast Points

Pacific Northwest, give this a try.

1 14.75-oz can red salmon, deboned
1 15-oz can green beans, drained
2 cups milk
3 Tbsp flour
$^1/_2$ stick margarine ($^1/_4$ cup)
$^1/_4$ cup grated cheddar cheese
Toasted bread
Salt and pepper, to taste

Melt margarine in a foil skillet on a grate over hot coals. Gradually stir in flour to make a creamy paste. Add milk, cheese, salt, and pepper, stirring until thickened. Finally, add salmon and green beans. Cook until heated through. Serve on toast points. Serves 4.

Salmon and Potato Patties

Serve with creamed peas and pearl onions.

1 14.75-oz can red salmon, boned and drained

2 cups mashed potatoes (already prepared and cooled)

1 egg, slightly beaten

1 onion, finely chopped

$^1/_4$ tsp salt

$^1/_4$ tsp pepper

3 Tbsp margarine

Combine salmon, mashed potatoes, egg, onion, salt, and pepper; mix well. Form into patties. Melt margarine in a foil skillet on a grate over medium-hot coals. Add salmon patties and fry until heated through and golden brown on both sides. Serves 4.

Stuffed Trout Sesame

8 pan-size trout fillets, boned

1 cup bread crumbs

3 Tbsp sesame seeds

4 green onions

$^1/_2$ tsp seasoning salt

$^1/_4$ cup margarine, melted

3 Tbsp grated parmesan cheese

$^1/_2$ tsp paprika

Spray a double thickness sheet of heavy duty aluminum foil with non-stick cooking spray. Arrange 4 fish fillets on foil. Combine next four ingredients. Pour in margarine and toss to mix. Divide stuffing, place on top of each fillet. Then top with remaining fillets; sprinkle with parmesan cheese. Seal pocket; place on grate over medium-hot coals. Cook 18-20 minutes, turning once, or until fish flakes easily with fork. Remove fish. Sprinkle with paprika and serve. Serves 4.

Trout Parmesan

Mountain States, take notice.

8 (8-10-oz) trout fillets
1 cup fine dry bread crumbs
$1/_2$ cup parmesan cheese
2 eggs
$1/_2$ cup milk
Vegetable oil
Salt and pepper, to taste

Beat eggs and milk until well mixed; set aside. In another bowl, combine bread crumbs, cheese, salt, and pepper; set aside.

Heat vegetable oil in a foil skillet on a grate over hot coals. Dip fillets first in beaten egg, then dredge with bread crumb mixture. Fry fillets until golden brown and fish flakes with a fork. Serves 4.

Wayne's Favorite Salmon Steak with Cilantro

4 salmon steaks
$1/_4$ cup cilantro, chopped
$1/_2$ cup sun-dried tomatoes
$1/_3$ cup gr. onions, thinly sliced
Salt and pepper, to taste

Soak sun-dried tomatoes in water for 15 minutes, drain, and set aside.

Place salmon on large sheet (double thickness) of aluminum foil. Cover with cilantro, green onions, and rehydrated tomatoes. Seal foil and place on a grate over hot coals, salmon side down.

Cook for 20 to 25 minutes. Using hot pads or oven mitts, carefully open foil pocket and check salmon for doneness. Fully cooked salmon will flake easily when tested with a fork. Serves 4.

Vegetables

Best Ever
Baked Beans

Makes a nice accompaniment to "Double Wrapped Dogs".

2 15-oz cans pork and beans
1.2-oz pkg dry onion soup mix
$^1/_2$ cup ketchup
$^3/_4$ cup brown sugar

Combine all ingredients in a foil pot on a grate over medium-hot coals.
Cover and simmer for 45 minutes. Uncover and cook for an additional
15 minutes. Serves 4-6.

Buttered Spuds and Cobs

12 new potatoes
4 fresh ears of corn
4 small onions
3 Tbsp margarine

Place all ingredients on a double thickness of heavy duty aluminum
foil and seal loosely.

Place the foil pocket on a grate over hot coals. Cook for 30 minutes, or
until potatoes are tender. Serves 4.

Cauliflower with Double Topper
Equally good with broccoli.

1 medium head cauliflower
4 slices processed cheese
$1/_4$ cup pimentos, chopped
2 Tbsp water

Place the cauliflower on a double thickness of heavy duty aluminum foil, and sprinkle with water. Seal the foil loosely around the cauliflower.

Place the foil pocket on a grate over hot coals. Steam for 15 to 20 minutes, or until heated through. Carefully open the foil pocket and top the cauliflower with cheese and pimentos. Continue cooking until the cheese begins to melt. Serves 4-6.

Cauliflower and Tomato Casserole
Even picky eaters love it

1 medium head of cauliflower
1 14.5-oz can diced tomatoes
1 Tbsp onion, finely diced
Salt and pepper, to taste
$1/_4$ cup freshly grated Parmesan cheese
$1/_2$ cup cheese crackers, crushed

Wash cauliflower, remove leaves, and break into florets. Cook, covered with a small amount of water, in a foil pot on a grate over hot coals until crisp-tender. Drain water. Place cooked cauliflower in a shallow foil pan. Add tomatoes, onion, salt, and pepper. Sprinkle with freshly grated Parmesan cheese and top with cheese crackers. Cover pan and cook on a grate over medium-hot coals for 10-15 minutes, or until heated through. Serves 4-6.

Corn Stuffed Tomatoes

4 tomatoes, insides removed
1 15-oz can whole corn, drained
2 Tbsp green onions, sliced
1 Tbsp pimentoes, chopped
2 Tbsp parmesan cheese, grated

Combine corn, green onions, and pimentos. Stuff gently into the tomatoes and place on a double thickness of heavy duty aluminum foil. Seal the foil pocket, then set on a cooking grate over medium-hot coals. Cook for 15 to 20 minutes, or until tomatoes are heated through. Before serving, sprinkle with parmesan cheese. Serves 4.

Fried Sweet Potato Cakes

Serve with applesauce and you will give sweet potatoes the respect they deserve.

4 small sweet potatoes, pared
2 eggs
2 Tbsp flour
Salt and pepper, to taste
Vegetable oil

Grate sweet potatoes into a foil bowl; drain off liquid. Beat eggs into the potatoes, stir in the flour, and season with salt and pepper.

Meanwhile, heat vegetable oil in another foil skillet on a grate over hot coals. Carefully drop spoonfuls of sweet potato mixture into the hot oil. Fry until edges are crisp and lightly browned. Turn, and brown other side. Drain on paper toweling. Serves 4-6.

Gardeny Spaghetti

1 16-oz pkg spaghetti
1 5-oz pkg cream cheese
$^1/_2$ cup milk
2 tomatoes, chopped
1 cup carrots, shredded
$^3/_4$ cup green onions, sliced
1 Tbsp parsley, chopped
2 cloves garlic, minced
2 Tbsp margarine
$^1/_2$ cup grated parmesan cheese
Salt and pepper, to taste

Prepare spaghetti according to package directions in a foil pot on a grate over hot coals. Melt margarine in a foil skillet on a grate over hot coals. Add cream cheese and milk, stirring until creamy and smooth. Add remaining ingredients and cook until tender. Serve over spaghetti. Serves 6.

Great Combo Fried Veggies

4 medium potatoes, peeled
1 medium onion
2 carrots, pared
1 7-oz can corn, drained
2 eggs
2 Tbsp flour
Salt and pepper, to taste
Vegetable oil

Grate potatoes, onion, and carrots into a foil bowl. Drain off liquid and stir in corn. Beat in eggs and flour, and season with salt and pepper.

Heat vegetable oil in another foil skillet on a grate over hot coals. Carefully drop spoonfuls of potato mixture into the hot oil. Fry until edges are crisp and lightly browned. Turn, and brown the other side. Drain on paper toweling. Serves 4-6.

The Great Coated Potato Bake

4 potatoes, cubed
1.2-oz pkg dry onion soup mix
1 Tbsp vegetable oil
OR
4 potatoes, cubed
1 1.5-oz pkg taco seasoning
1 Tbsp vegetable oil
OR
4 potatoes, cubed
$^1/_2$ cup parmesan cheese, grated
1 Tbsp vegetable oil
OR
4 potatoes, cubed
$^1/_2$ cup cajun spices
1 Tbsp vegetable oil
OR
4 potatoes, cubed
1 pkg dry brown gravy mix
1 Tbsp vegetable oil

Mix 1 Tbsp vegetable oil with one of the seasoning blends. Place in a brown paper bag along with the potatoes; shake to coat.

Arrange coated potatoes on a double thickness of heavy duty aluminum foil and seal. Place the foil pockets on a grate over hot coals. Cook 20 to 25 minutes, or until potatoes are fork tender. Serves 4-6.

Honey Cashew Green Beans

A good side with any meal.

1 15-oz can green beans, drained

2 Tbsp honey

$^1/_4$ cup orange marmalade

$^1/_4$ cup cashews

Salt and pepper, to taste

Place green beans on a double thickness of heavy duty aluminum foil. Spoon honey and orange marmalade on top, then season with salt and pepper. Seal the foil pocket.

Place on a grate over medium-hot coals and cook for 15 minutes, or until heated through. Before serving, sprinkle cashews on top. Serves 4.

Lima Bean Casserole

The kids will like these limas.

2 15-oz cans baby lima beans, drained

1 15-oz can creamed corn

1 Tbsp margarine

1 small can french fried onions

$^1/_4$ cup slivered almonds

Salt and pepper, to taste

Combine beans, corn, margarine, one-half can french fried onions, salt, and pepper in a foil pot on a grate over medium-hot coals. Heat for 15 minutes, stirring often.

Top with almonds and remaining french fried onions. Continue cooking for 10 minutes. Serves 6.

Mixed Veggie Casserole

1 15-oz can mixed vegetables, drained
1 3-oz pkg cream cheese, softened
2 cups milk
3 Tbsp flour
$\frac{1}{2}$ stick margarine ($\frac{1}{4}$ cup)
Salt and pepper, to taste

Topping:
$\frac{1}{2}$ cup grated cheddar cheese
3 Tbsp margarine
2 slices toast, cubed

Melt margarine in a foil pot on a grate over medium-hot coals. Gradually stir in flour to make a creamy paste. Add milk, cream cheese, salt, and pepper; stir until thickened. Add vegetables; heat for 10 minutes. Sprinkle on grated cheese and toast cubes that have been tossed with 3 Tbsp melted margarine. Continue heating until cheese begins to melt. Serves 4-6.

Nutty Brussels Sprouts
Crunchy and flavorful

32 fresh brussels sprouts
4 Tbsp slivered almonds
3 Tbsp water
2 tsp Dijon mustard

Combine all ingredients on a double thickness of heavy duty aluminum foil; seal pocket. Set foil pocket on a grate over medium-hot coals and cook for 20-25 minutes, or until brussels sprouts are tender. Serves 4.

Rainbow Peppers

A terrific way to serve those
wonderful summer peppers.

1 red pepper, cut into strips
1 yellow pepper, cut into strips
1 green pepper, cut into strips
2 onions, cut into rings
2 Tbsp margarine
1 Tbsp brown sugar

Melt margarine in a foil skillet on a grate over medium-hot coals. Add remaining ingredients and cook, stirring often, until peppers and onions are tender. Serves 4.

Raisins 'N Carrots

10 carrots, sliced
$^1/_4$ cup brown sugar, packed
1 Tbsp cornstarch
$^1/_4$ cup water
$^1/_4$ cup raisins

Combine all ingredients on a double thickness of heavy duty aluminum foil; seal pocket. Place on a grate over medium-hot coals and cook for 30-40 minutes, or until carrots are tender. Serves 4.

Steamed - Fresh from the Garden
Loaded with vitamins and minerals.

2 cups cauliflower florets
4 stalks broccoli
1 cup green beans
4 carrots
$1/2$ summer squash, pulp removed
4 small onions
3 Tbsp margarine
2 Tbsp water
Salt and pepper, to taste

Place all ingredients on a double thickness of heavy duty aluminum foil. Seal the foil loosely around the vegetables. Place the foil pocket on a grate over hot coals. Steam 25 to 30 minutes, or until all vegetables are tender. Serves 4-6.

Steamed Ranch Potatoes

4 medium baking potatoes, quartered lengthwise
1 2-oz pkg dry ranch dressing
$1/4$ cup margarine, melted
$1/2$ cup sour cream
$1/4$ cup green onions, sliced
1 tomato, chopped

Melt margarine in a foil skillet on a grate over medium hot coals. Pour over quartered potatoes, then dredge potatoes with dry ranch dressing. Arrange potatoes on a double thickness of heavy duty aluminum foil and seal pocket. Place the foil pocket on a grate over medium-hot coals. Steam for 20 minutes, or until potatoes are fork tender. Just before serving, top with sour cream, green onions, and tomatoes. Serves 4.

Stuffed Potatoes
Medley of flavors

2 large baking potatoes, washed
$^1/_4$ cup sour cream
1 5-oz can ham, drained
1 small can corn, drained
2 green onions, sliced
Dash tabasco sauce
$^1/_2$ cup cheddar cheese, shredded

Wrap potatoes in aluminum foil and bake on grate over medium-hot coals until fork tender. Let cool. Cut each potato lengthwise; scoop out centers leaving a $^1/_4$" shell. Mash potatoes and sour cream until well mixed. Stir in ham, corn, onions, and tabasco sauce. Divide mixture evenly between potato shells; sprinkle with cheese. Place back on grate and heat until cheese melts. Serves 4.

Sweet Onion Casserole
Mouth watering appeal

4 vidalia onions, sliced $^1/_4$" thick
$^1/_4$ cup margarine
$^1/_4$ cup sour cream
$^3/_4$ cup parmesan cheese
12 "Ritz" crackers, crushed

Saute onions in margarine in a foil skillet on a grate over medium-hot coals until tender. Remove from heat; stir in sour cream. Spoon half of the mixture into a greased foil pan made with 2 thicknesses of heavy duty aluminum foil. Sprinkle with cheese and top with remaining onions. Cover with crackers. Bake uncovered in a reflector oven for 35-40 minutes, rotating pan 2-3 times.Serves 4-6.

Sweet Potatoes 'N Honey

4 small sweet potatoes, cut in half
4 Tbsp margarine
$^1/_2$ cup honey
$^1/_4$ cup brown sugar
$^1/_4$ cup raisins

Place all ingredients on a double thickness of heavy duty aluminum foil and seal. Place the foil pocket on a grate over hot coals. Cook 30 to 45 minutes, or until potatoes are fork tender. Serves 4.

Note: Add $^1/_4$ cup chopped pecans to really punch up the flavor.

You'll Want Them Again Potato Cakes
Melt-in-your-mouth good

4 medium potatoes, peeled
1 medium onion
2 eggs
2 Tbsp flour
Salt and pepper, to taste
Vegetable oil

Grate potatoes and onion into a foil bowl; drain off liquid. Beat eggs into the potatoes, stir in flour, and season with salt and pepper. Meanwhile, heat vegetable oil in another foil skillet on a grate over hot coals. Carefully drop spoonfuls of potato mixture into the hot oil. Fry until edges are crisp and lightly browned. Turn, and brown the other side. Drain on paper toweling. Serves 4-6.

Desserts

Apples with Caramel Sauce

Irresistible treat

2 Tbsp margarine
3 Tbsp brown sugar, packed
$1/2$ tsp apple pie spice
3 large tart apples, cored and sliced
$1/4$ cup English walnuts, chopped
$1/4$ cup caramel topping

Melt margarine in a foil skillet on a grate over medium-hot coals. Stir in brown sugar and apple pie spice; add apples and walnuts. Cook, stirring occasionally for 10-12 minutes or until apples are tender. Remove from heat, divide into 4 servings and drizzle with caramel topping. Serves 4.

Apple and Raisin Crisp

A perfect ending to any meal.

6 tart apples, cored and sliced
$1/2$ cup raisins
$2/3$ cup brown sugar

Topping:
$1/2$ stick margarine, softened
2 Tbsp sugar
$1/2$ tsp cinnamon
1 cup biscuit mix

Spread apples over the bottom of a foil pan. Cover with raisins and brown sugar. Mix remaining ingredients until crumbly and sprinkle over apples.

Cover with foil and put on a grate over medium hot coals. Cook until apples are tender. Serves 6.

Blackberry Breeze

One of our favorite Misouri State Parks is Weston Bend State Park, near Weston, Missouri on the banks of the Missouri river. From mid-July through mid-August wild blackberries are abundantly ripe for harvest. The campground is always full during this period of time.

2 cups fresh blackberries, washed
$3^{1}/_{2}$ cups milk
1 pkg (3.4 oz) instant vanilla pudding
4 sections graham crackers, crushed

Pour milk and pudding mix into a quart size zip-lock plastic bag; shake vigorously for 2 minutes.

Meanwhile, wash blackberries and divide into 4 serving bowls. To serve, spoon desired amount of pudding mixture over berries and sprinkle on crushed graham crackers. Serves 4.

Blackberry Cobbler, Weston Bend Style

Dedicated to head Ranger, Nancy

4 cups fresh blackberries, washed
$^2/_3$ cup sugar
$^2/_3$ cup biscuit mix
3 Tbsp brown sugar, packed
$^1/_4$ cup margarine
3 Tbsp milk

Combine blackberries and sugar in a 8" x 8" aluminum baking pan; set aside. In a foil bowl, combine biscuit mix and brown sugar; cut in margarine until crumbly. Stir in milk just until blended. Drop by spoonful onto blackberries.

Place pan on a grate over medium-hot coals; cover with an aluminum foil tent and bake for 20-25 minutes or until top is golden brown and filling is bubbly. Serves 6-8.

Can't Be Easier Peach Crisp

A real people pleaser

1 can (1 lb 5 oz) peach pie filling
1 cup honey almond oat cereal
1 Tbsp margarine
$^1/_4$ tsp cinnamon
$^1/_4$ tsp nutmeg

Heat pie filling in a foil pan on a grate over medium-hot coals. Pour into a serving container.

Meanwhile, combine remaining ingredients in a foil skillet; place on grate over medium-hot coals and stir for 5-6 minutes, or until heated through. Sprinkle cereal mixture over peaches and serve warm. Serves 4-6.

Colorful Pears and Cranberries

Pear lovers delight

For each pear, you'll need:

1 Tbsp brown sugar

3 Tbsp jellied cranberry sauce

Wash and core pears, making sure not to cut through the bottom. Fill the cavity with brown sugar and cranberries. Place on a double thickness of heavy duty aluminum foil, spoon remaining cranberry sauce around pears and seal the pocket.

Place the foil pocket on a grate over medium hot coals. Cook 20 to 25 minutes, or until pears are tender

Crispy Apple Crunch

4 tart apples, sliced

$^1/_3$ cup sugar

$^1/_4$ cup raisins

$^1/_2$ tsp cinnamon

Topping:

$^1/_2$ cup uncooked quick oats

3 Tbsp pecans, finely chopped

2 Tbsp brown sugar

2 Tbsp margarine

Place combined apple mixture on a double thickness of heavy duty aluminum foil. Cover with mixed topping and seal.

Put the foil pocket on a grate over medium hot coals. Cook for 20 to 25 minutes, or until apples are tender. Serves 4.

Delightfully Crunchy Bananas

They'll want this one at home, too.

4 bananas
2 eggs, beaten
1 cup corn flakes, crushed
$^1/_2$ cup honey
Vegetable oil

Heat oil in a foil pan on a grate over medium hot coals. Meanwhile, cut bananas in half. Dip first in beaten egg, then in crushed corn flakes.

Fry bananas in heated oil until golden and crispy. Drain on paper toweling. Before serving, drizzle honey over the bananas. Serves 4.

Grandmother's Fried Apple Pies

Our thanks to grandmothers everywhere.

Filling:
$1^1/_4$ cups tart apples, cored, peeled and sliced
$^1/_2$ cup sugar
$^1/_2$ tsp cinnamon
$^1/_4$ tsp nutmeg
$^1/_4$ cup raisins (optional)

Pastry:
2 cups flour
$^1/_4$ tsp salt
$^2/_3$ cup shortening
$^1/_4$ cup water

Combine filling ingredients in a foil bowl; set aside.

Mix together flour and salt. Cut in shortening and add just enough water to make a firm dough.

Roll dough out onto a floured surface and cut out four inch circles. Place filling down the center of each circle, fold over, and seal with the tines of a fork.

Meanwhile, heat oil in a foil skillet on a grate over hot coals. Fry pies until golden brown, remove, and drain on paper toweling. Sprinkle with sugar before serving, if desired. Makes 8 to 10 pies.

Mountain Man's Apple Cobbler
Flatlanders will like it too.

2 15.5-oz cans or jars applesauce
$^1/_2$ cup red hots
1 7.5-oz can refrigerator biscuits (10 count)
1 Tbsp margarine
Cinnamon/sugar mixture

Combine applesauce, red hots, and margarine in a foil pot on a grate over hot coals. Bring to a simmer.

Meanwhile, cut biscuits into fourths. Roll each piece into a ball shape and coat with cinnamon/sugar mixture. Drop biscuits on top of simmering applesauce, cover with foil, and cook until biscuits are done. Serves 6.

Nutty Good Apples
Crunchy good

6 tart apples, cored
$3/4$ cup granola
3 Tbsp margarine
$1/2$ cup brown sugar
$1/2$ cup raisins
$1/4$ cup peanuts, chopped

When coring the apples, do not break through the bottom.

Combine granola, brown sugar, raisins, and peanuts. Mix well, then stuff into apples. Top each apple with $1/2$ Tbsp margarine.

Place apples on a double thickness of heavy duty aluminum foil and seal. Put the foil pockets on a grate over medium-hot coals. Cook for 20 to 25 minutes, or until apples are tender. Serves 6.

P-Nutty Good Bananas
Parents and kids alike will enjoy this sweet treat.

4 bananas
2 graham crackers, crushed
$3/4$ cup chunky peanut butter

Warm peanut butter in a foil pan on a grate over medium hot coals.

Slice bananas, and divide into four serving-sized portions. Drizzle warmed peanut butter over fruit, then sprinkle with crushed graham crackers. Serves 4.

Rocky Road Bananas

Sinfully good.

4 bananas
$^1/_2$ cup chocolate syrup
$^3/_4$ cup marshmallow creme
$^1/_4$ cup chopped nuts

Cut bananas in half lengthwise. Drizzle chocolate syrup over the fruit, then top with marshmallow creme and nuts. Serves 4.

S'Mores in the '90s

Sweet ending to a perfect day.

Marshmallows
Graham crackers
Canned icing of your choice

Spread icing on graham crackers and set aside. Brown marshmallows on a stick over hot coals. Set on top of the icing. Place another graham cracker on top and enjoy a very traditional campfire treat.

Strawberries and Bananas
Always a good combination.

4 bananas
2 graham crackers, crushed
$^3/_4$ cup strawberry preserves

Heat strawberry preserves in foil pan on grate over medium hot coals. Slice bananas and divide into four portions. Drizzle warmed strawberry preserves over bananas and sprinkle with crushed graham crackers. Serves 4.

Strawberry Streusel Squares
Exciting outdoor treat

$1^1/_2$ cups biscuit mix
1 cup quick oats
$^3/_4$ cup sugar
$^1/_2$ tsp cinnamon
$^1/_4$ tsp nutmeg
$^1/2$ cup margarine, melted
1 cup strawberry preserves
$^1/_4$ cup walnuts, chopped
$^1/_2$ tsp salt

Combine biscuit mix, oats, sugar, cinnamon and nutmeg in foil bowl; beat in melted margarine until ingredients are moistened. Reserve half of this biscuit mixture for topping.

Pat remaining mixture into a greased 8" x 8" aluminum foil pan. Spread strawberry preserves on top to within 1/2" of edges. Combine walnuts with remaining the mixture and sprinkle over preserves.

Place the pan on a grate over medium-hot coals, cover with aluminum foil and bake for 30-35 minutes or until lightly browned. Cool before cutting into squares.

Upside Easy
Pineapple Cake

4 pineapple slices
4 tsp pineapple juice
8 tsp brown sugar, packed
4 tsp margarine
4 slices pound cake

Arrange pineapple slices in an 8" x 8" aluminum foil pan; pour in pineapple juice. Top each slice with 2 tsp brown sugar and 1 tsp margarine. Center pound cake on each pineapple slice.

Place pan on a grate over medium-hot coals. Heat until hot and bubbly and cake feels warm to the touch. When done, invert pan on serving plate. Serves 4.

Index